200p.

CW01082035

Visually handicapped children
and young people

Special needs in education

SERIES EDITOR
Ron Gulliford, Professor of Education,
University of Birmingham

Visually handicapped children and young people

Elizabeth K. Chapman

Department of Special Education
University of Birmingham

Routledge & Kegan Paul
London, Henley and Boston

371·911

First published in 1978
by Routledge & Kegan Paul Ltd
39 Store Street,
London WC1E 7DD,
Broadway House,
Newtown Road,
Henley-on-Thames,
Oxon RG9 1EN and
9 Park Street,
Boston, Mass. 02108, USA
Set in Baskerville by
Computacomp (UK) Ltd, Fort William, Scotland
and printed in Great Britain by
Unwin Brothers Ltd
The Gresham Press
Old Woking, Surrey
A member of the Staples Printing Group
© Elizabeth K. Chapman 1978

British Library Cataloguing in Publication Data

Chapman, Elizabeth K

    Visually handicapped children and
    young people. – (Special needs in education).
    1. Blind – Education
    I. Title II. Series
    371.9′11   HV1626   78–40326

ISBN 0 7100 8878 7

In memory of Myfanwy Williams
a great teacher

Contents

Series editor's preface

This series of books on special educational needs will be concerned with the practice of special and remedial education whether in ordinary or special schools, and with findings and implications of research and with the discussion of organization and provision. The series aims to provide informed accounts of the needs of different groups of handicapped pupils and how these needs may be met by appropriate teaching, therapy and care.

There is a considerable body of knowledge and a range of special methods and aids available to those who teach blind or partially sighted children. While this account is primarily intended for those who teach or who are training to teach visually handicapped children, the book will also be of help to other teachers, advisers and educational psychologists since children with visual handicaps may be found in special schools and units for children with other major handicaps; particularly the physically and the mentally handicapped and also in ordinary schools. The needs of visually handicapped children and what kinds of help and specialist advice are or should be available require to be more widely known.

But it is by no means just a book for those directly concerned with schools. Effective education and care of the visually handicapped – from pre-school through to the post-school years – calls upon the well-co-ordinated efforts of many people – not least the parents, counsellors, doctors, social workers, administrators as well as members of local authorities and voluntary organizations. The more everyone understands the whole task the better their particular contributions can be.

Although provisions for the education and other special requirements of visually handicapped children and young people are well-established in this country there are many new ideas and developments taking shape at the present time. As a former teacher of visually handicapped children, as a tutor of the only course in England for training teachers of visually handicapped children and as someone who has held office in organizations of teachers of the partially sighted as well as the blind, Elizabeth Chapman is well qualified to describe the present situation in what is in fact the first British book on this subject. More important, Elizabeth Chapman is able to communicate her own enthusiasm for this branch of special education and her own deep commitment to the development of this work.

Ron Gulliford

Acknowledgments

My thanks are due to Professor Ronald Gulliford for his encouragement and wise guidance as Editor of this series. Among the colleagues who have kindly read and commented constructively on the text I must especially thank Dr M. J. Tobin, Director of the Research Centre for the Education of the Visually Handicapped at the University of Birmingham, and Mr B. Hechle, Honorary Registrar of the College of Teachers of the Blind. Mr I. C. Fraser FRCSE most helpfully scrutinized the section concerned with eye problems, and the diagrammatic representation was produced by J. A. Greene ARCA advised by Cicely Chapman-Andresen Ph.D; Mrs Jennifer Whittaker has typed the script with speed and efficiency. Finally, my students past and present, have by their enthusiasm and enquiry, helped to contribute fresh thinking about the needs of visually handicapped children.

I Visually handicapped children – who are they?

Nature and implications of visual handicap

Because he is not wearing glasses, many people do not realize at first just how little he can see. Should he learn braille or try reading print with his book held up near to his face? Does he need to go to a special school, or can he get the help he really needs in an ordinary class? Can he manage to do the same school subjects as other children, and perhaps pass the same exams, or will he tend to be left behind in his school work, missing out on sport, standing on the sidelines while the others play football? Questions like these arise when one is considering the needs of a severely visually handicapped child whose parents are looking ahead with some anxiety, perhaps wondering about his chances of undertaking further education, or even finding a job that suits him after leaving school. They notice already that some situations are difficult for him; perhaps he cannot make out the number on a bus, or recognize the face of a friend across the street, but he resents being helped too much and likes to get on with his hobby of making model aircraft in his own time, and in his own way; at school his teachers may wonder if too much is being done for him or too little.

Many school tasks are dependent on vision, and a child may experience difficulties if he cannot use his sight with ease and efficiency; in the ordinary classroom situation it is generally assumed that the pupil can see clearly at a distance and in the near environment, and that he can maintain binocular vision for work at his desk, reading, drawing, examining an insect, and then switch to a further range in looking up at the more distantly placed blackboard, or wall-mounted diagram. He will need to rely on his longer distance vision in the cricket match and to change fixation and yet maintain his visual concentration throughout the varied and changing activities of the school day.

A diminished visual field may be evident as apparent clumsiness and seemingly poor eye-hand co-ordination; difficulties in seeing clearly may present themselves in the unusual position or movements that a child shows while working, such as tilting his head forward, whilst facial grimaces such as frowning or squinting can in some cases indicate sight problems. Actions indicating discomfort such as rubbing the eyes frequently, or excessive blinking and complaints of dizziness, headache and nausea, covering one eye with the hand, and poking the corner of it with the finger are all signs listed by Marshall (1969a) as indicating the possible presence of visual dysfunction. Of course manifestations of this kind may originate from causes unconnected with visual problems, but their persistence as part of a child's behaviour could indicate a situation in which it would be wise to seek ophthalmological investigation. Choice of activities has sometimes been linked with visual capacity and comfort; is it the case that the child who does not enjoy games may sometimes have the fallible sight that makes it hard for him to succeed in these activities? Lack of motivation, tiredness and apathy may be more cogent reasons for such an aversion, but the part played by sight in achieving success in such areas needs to be understood by the teacher.

It is, of course, late if a child's difficulties in seeing are picked up only during his school career, and much more useful if his school placement is the result of considered decision after his visual condition has been assessed and recognition given to possible sight problems.

Discovery of visual handicap in children

Health services are organized to provide for the regular and continuous observation of children's development from infancy through the school years. The first indication of visual impairment in a young child may become evident during this process of developmental screening, in which procedure an attempt is made to determine the handicapped child's level of functioning in sensory, physical, intellectual and communication areas. Broadly based assessment of this kind is likely to involve the community physician, paediatrician, educational psychologist, and medical social worker. The aim of such screening is to detect the assets and defects of the child after careful examination, and as a result of the interpretation of the findings appropriate intervention in the form of medical treatment and prescriptions and educational placement should follow. It is essential in the case of a handicapped child whose development may show a disturbed or uneven pattern that his abilities should be sampled in a variety of ways. Current approaches lay stress on the coding in functional terms of the disabilities of children with multiple handicaps. Qualitative estimates of the child's capacities in the area of physical and motor functioning as well as in behaviour and communication will be made. Severe visual handicap may affect these functions, for example in the handling and recognition of toys, or in the ability to perform quite simple tasks effectively.

Developmental screening is only one of the routes leading to the discovery of visual handicap since the general practitioner or school medical officer may refer a child for further investigation perhaps after a parent, teacher or health visitor has noted and reported the fact that the child seems to have difficulties in seeing; illness or accident may have indicated that sight problems could have contributed to difficulties in school.

Developmental screening, assessment, and ascertainment

The whole process of determining which children will need special education, either in a special school or in an ordinary school with supportive services, includes the three stages of discovery, diagnosis and assessment. There is the initial stage of finding out which children have disabilities which should be followed by the determination of the extent, the causes and the nature of such disabilities. After this discovery and diagnosis, the effects of these on the functioning of the child require assessment and consideration must be given to the nature of any special education that will be needed. In the UK a statement of what is involved in these three steps of discovery, diagnosis and assessment is contained in Circular No. 2/75 issued by the Department of Education and Science (1975) and No. 21/75 Welsh Office (1975). This sets out the procedure for the use of Forms SE1–6 if a decision is made that a child may need special education after a full diagnosis has been made of his disabilities, and after his development and his skills have been assessed. It is stressed that medical examination should precede psychological assessment, and that parents should be brought into consultation even before initial medical and psychological investigations are commenced. If the sequel to the recommendation is that the child is entered for a special school or unit, his parents should be encouraged to visit this. The six Forms SE1–6 are the current instrument by which the statutory requirement of Section 34 of the Education Act of 1944 are implemented, mainly in fulfilling the duty of every local authority to ascertain what children in their area require special educational treatment, and to comply with the request of any parents for a child over two years of age to have a medical examination. Forms SE1–3 are completed by the child's teacher, the school doctor and an educational psychologist. Form SE4 incorporates a summary and action sheet which describes the needs of a child who requires special education, and Form SE5 contains the essential elements of the previously used Handicapped Pupils Form 1 being in effect a description of the handicap. Form SE5 records the whole of the medical examination. Form SE6 is an up-dated version of the formerly used Handicapped Pupils Form 6, and relates to the particular circumstances of parents who are serving in the Forces. Thus it will be seen that the first three forms record the educational, medical and psychological data which should be filled in first. Recommendations are then considered and the descriptive list now based more upon educational needs than on diagnostic categories is filled in appropriately on Form SE4. The nature and extent of the disability is recorded on Form SE5 after the facts have been determined by medical examination.

A clear and complete picture of the medical conditions will be contributed by the paediatrician to his colleagues, whilst the psychologist will be concerned to assess the child's present level of mental functioning and to attempt to discover something of his basic level of intellectual potential. There are problems here with regard to the assessment of visually handicapped children, since cognizance must be taken of the limiting effect on performance of impaired or absent sight.

The school doctor, the educational psychologist and the child's teacher all have a contribution to make to assessment when the child reaches school age, but initial assessment is of considerable importance since one of its sequels may be a recommendation with regard to the kind of school considered most well-suited to the handicapped child.

Appropriate educational placement may be one of the most crucial factors in the eventual school success and social adjustment of the visually handicapped child, with the implication that the assessment which guides such placement should not only be early and consultative, but on-going with the opportunity for review. Although research is needed to investigate the magnitude of the problem, it is a cause for concern that heads of special schools for the blind and partially sighted still complain of the late transfers into special provision of visually handicapped children who have failed in educational attainment in schools for the sighted and have accumulated a backlog of failure, before action is taken to help them resolve their problems in the classroom. The extent to which such failures are due to visual problems or to a compound of these together with other factors is a question that needs skilled and patient unravelling in individual cases.

A complete profile of the child's functioning and behaviour will include a consideration of any visual disabilities and, in the increasing recognition of the value of team assessment, many psychologists today would wish to supplement the findings from standardized developmental and intelligence tests by observing the responses of visually handicapped children to learning and play situations, whilst teachers should be able to contribute to the sum of relevant information by their own observations. It can be the teacher who is in a favourable position to indicate the verbal communication levels of the child over a period of time, citing whether he vocalizes his needs and thoughts, and noting if his speech seems meaningful, with an awareness of concepts, or if it seems to be just rote memory and repetition. The blind or poorly sighted child may receive and play with toys in an unusual way that appeals to his non-visual senses, or on the other hand his play may be very like that of sighted children. Kenyon (1967) suggests that the recording of observations of this kind may help to round out the total picture of the visually handicapped child's functioning, and indicate whether he enjoys toys that other children of his own age would be expected to play with, whether he has a short attention span and is distractable, or whether he plays purposefully; his interaction with other children and with adults must also be noted, and it is vital to observe his ability to move about actively in and out of doors as this is a crucial factor in his readiness for school.

The results of tests and of observational records of this kind are useful indications guiding decisions towards appropriate treatment and educational provision, but the accurate diagnosis of sight problems may have medical implications, demanding the expert experience and knowledge of a consultant ophthalmologist.

Registration of blindness and of partial sight

If a defect of sight is diagnosed the child may be registered as blind or partially sighted; such registration, which is voluntary rather than statutory, can only be made on Form BD8 by a consultant ophthalmologist to whom the appropriate form is made available by the Social Services Department. This standard form developed from the registration form devised in 1920 under the Blind Persons Act when there was only one form of visual handicap recognized for either adults or children – that of blindness. By 1933 the Form had been considerably adapted, and a further revision was undertaken in 1968 so that it now includes information on visual acuity and field of vision, as well as age of onset of the condition. The clinical assessment includes prognosis and relevant information with regard to family history. Form BD8 has a section for recommendations relating to treatment, and in the case of a child from 0 to 16 years of age the consultant ophthalmologist completing the Form has the task of recommending that education should either be in a special school for the blind, a special school for the partially sighted or in an ordinary school with suitable modifications. It is, however, stated that the final decision with regard to the educational recommendation must be taken by the local education authority.

Fine (1975) notes anomalies in the educational recommendations entered in BD8 Forms completed and returned to the Department of Health and Social Security in a sample scrutiny from April to December 1973, and refers to the criticism of this Form in the report of the Vernon Committee on the Education of the Visually Handicapped (DES, 1972) which questions its use in educational assessment and considers that it places too much emphasis on visual acuity, drawing too rigid a distinction between blind, partially sighted and normally sighted children. In predicting further revisions Fine (op. cit.) foresees that no distinction will be required between blindness and partial sight and that educational placement should result from a multi-disciplinary team assessment. The consultant ophthalmologist provides essential information, but it is unrealistic to expect him to have to make the total decision with regard to educational placement as well.

Measurement of visual acuity

Harcourt (1975) gives a detailed description of clinical ophthalmic assessment in visually handicapped children, noting that difficulty in communication with a young subject increases the reliance on objective methods of examination, although information from parents may help to augment this. In the early stages, generally before the age of three (although developmental factors preclude firm reference to chronological age) the child will be unable to co-operate, requiring completely objective examination. The second stage is described as one in which the child is co-operative but illiterate, and able to understand only easy instructions which may be used in simple subjective tests of function so that objective methods of gaining information must still largely be used. In the third stage the techniques of examination are much the same as those used for adults.

The most generally recognized measurement of vision, and one that figures on Form BD8, is the measurement of visual acuity as shown by testing on the Snellen Chart. In this procedure, each eye is tested separately, then both are tested together. Most people are familiar with this test as it is frequently a routine part of medical examinations. The specially designed chart, bearing clear black letters of diminishing size, should be placed on a well-lit, shadow-free wall. The subject being tested initially stands six metres away from the chart; reading the top line the subject calls out the names of the letters of decreasing size line by line; if he cannot complete the entire chart at the six-metre distance he will be told to move closer, at spaced intervals, and attempt to continue to recognize the letters. For subjects who cannot name letters the Illiterate E or Landolt Broken Ring test is used instead. The recorded measurement of visual acuity from this test has the appearance of a fraction. The lower figure which looks like the denominator is usually taken as 60 in the UK but in measurements of visual acuity lower than normal this figure may be reduced to 30, 18 or 6. In simplified terms the upper figure which has the appearance of the numerator of a fraction represents the distance from the chart at which the subject would have to stand in order to recognize what the normally fully sighted subject could recognize from a distance of six metres. For example, a child showing a visual acuity of 3/6 would have a much lower level of visual acuity than one showing 6/6 which represents the normal level. The Chart is turned over to show a comparable but different set of letters on the other side in order to avoid memorizing. In each case the size and angles of the configuration of the letter have been carefully worked out in order to permit exact measurement of acuity. The procedure is usually repeated with corrective lenses, and both scores entered on the Form with the description of corrected and uncorrected visual acuity.

For the teacher, observation of the way in which a child appears to use his vision is essential, since it is possible for children with comparable measured visual acuity to seem to be able to perform tasks demanding sight differently; for example, one child with a low acuity will attempt to read print whilst another will say he is unable to do so.

The measurement of visual acuity by means of the Snellen Chart can be difficult with young children, and a simplified and adapted form of it has been incorporated in Sheridan's Test for Young Children and Retardates, generally referred to as STYCAR.

Measurement of visual fields and of colour vision

Harcourt (1975) stresses the importance of thorough scrutiny of the contents of the eye by means of an ophthalmoscope, and the need to assess the extent of the fields of vision as well as the acuity of vision. Visually stimulating targets such as white or coloured balls, or possibly toys can be introduced from various directions into the periphery of the visual fields and response to these can be recorded.

At an age and developmental stage when co-operation in simple subjective tests can be expected it is recommended that

8

colour vision also should be tested with the American Optical Company Handy Rand Rittler test using simple symbols for matching with a key card. Harcourt considers this procedure more satisfactory than the well-known Ishihara tests, since the former test grades the severity of any deficiency in colour discrimination, and also gives attention to the blue-yellow as well as to the red-green rays of the spectrum.

Structure of the eye and some possible defects and diseases

In order to be able to interpret the child's medical records it is helpful for those concerned with the child, including his teacher, to be reminded of the structure of the eye and to have some understanding of the diseases and conditions that can give rise to visual impairment. In doing so he must not try to usurp the position of the doctor or consultant, but rather seek to increase his understanding of the child's problems. Detailed descriptions will of course be found in standard medical textbooks such as *Modern Ophthalmology* (Sorsby, 1972) and a particularly helpful guide for teachers is also contained in *Eyes and Education* (Smith and James, 1968); see Figure 1.

Normally, the function of accommodation and convergence

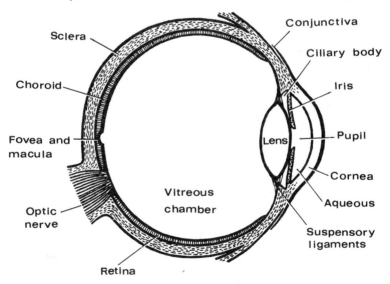

FIGURE 1   The eye

develops during infancy, culminating in the facility of seeing singly and clearly – seeing as we understand the term in a colloquial sense bears the implication of interpretation, a process which has to be learned, unaware as the subject may be of the learning process. It is difficult to gauge the extent to which the child simply accepts what he is seeing without being aware of the extent of any visual impairment which he may possess, unless it is a changing condition; he is unlikely to discuss in detail, or even at all, the difference between his own blurred or diminished vision and the clear and uninterrupted panorama of his fully sighted friend.

The eye is often likened to a camera, a crude analogy, but one which draws attention to the refractive quality of the lens and the light-sensitive quality of the retina. Anatomically, the eye may be described as a spherical sac with opaque walls except for the clear window-like cornea at the front. The contents of the eye are protected by the strong, white outer coating called the sclera which has an inner coating referred to as the choroid. This thickens towards the front of the eye, with the anterior portion of the uvea being visible as the coloured diaphragm, the iris, which surrounds the pupillary opening seen as a round black spot in the centre of the eye. Vernon Smith (1971) describes some of the developmental defects which can be seen affecting the eyes of children. For example, the pupil can have an almost keyhole shape referred to as a coloboma. The spherical shape of the eye is maintained by the content of transparent jelly-like substance referred to as the vitreous humour; the anterior chamber of the eye is separated from the larger posterior chamber by the crystalline lens, shaped like a convex disc. In children this lens is extremely flexible, enabling them to hold work at any distance from the eye, even at very close range without discomfort, since the elastic quality of the lens enables it to alter its shape and consequently its power of refraction easily. Advancing years decrease this ability until by middle age many normally sighted people need to wear glasses for reading to compensate for the decreased flexibility of the lens.

The lens and the convex, transparent cornea at the front of the eye act as refractors of light rays onto the retina – the thin lining at the back of the posterior chamber which is embedded with specialized cells, the rods and cones which enable it to function as a photosensitive screen. The sight of some children can be impaired by the presence of opacities in the lens. These are relatively soft and can often be broken up and extracted, but a number of hospital visits may be necessary for this. In addition to the frequent treatment sometimes necessary to deal with soft cataracts, a child can be in the unusual situation of having to come to terms with a better level of seeing than he has previously experienced. A 7-year-old girl in a school for blind and partially sighted children was encountered holding her sandal up close to her face and examining it minutely, gazing at it for almost a quarter of an hour. She had recently had successful treatment for cataract and appeared fascinated by the appearance of ordinary day-to-day objects that she must have previously seen very imperfectly. The relative prevalence of this condition is noted by Fine (1968) in her survey of 1,374 children in schools and classes for the partially sighted in England and Wales. In analysing the cause of defect among two groups of children, Group A consisting of those born between 1951 and 1955, and Group B consisting of those born between 1956 and 1960, she noted that cataract was the chief cause of visual defect in both groups. She also noted a strong hereditary factor, especially among the girls.

The regulating mechanism within the eye controlling pressure may be defective thus causing glaucoma; in its congenital form the enlargement of the eye thus induced gives rise to a bulging, often protruding eye referred to as bupthalmous from the Greek 'ox-eye'. It is not only a disfiguring condition, but one which children find uncomfortable and trying, often complaining of headache and pain.

Sometimes the inner layers of the eye are considered as an outpocketing of the brain, but the function of the brain in the seeing process is emphasized when we recall that the real image of what is seen is small and inverted.

The highly sensitive retina lining the back of the eye is embedded with rods and cones; uncommon cones can be the cause of colour blindness, sometimes discovered accidentally, as when a small boy depicted a strawberry as a greenish brown in his painting; his teacher laughed but recognition of the child's difficulty and identification of his problem was a sequel to this incident. The thickness of the retina varies, the most receptive area being shown as the macula or yellow spot, whilst the place at which the optic nerves (which cross at the optic chiasma) enter the eye, is sometimes referred to as the 'blind spot'. Diseases of the retina such as retinitis pigmentosa can cause a descrease in peripheral vision at some stages, a decreased visual field that has been referred to as giving the impression of a curtailed vista such as one sees when looking down the sights of a gun. Dim light also causes difficulties for children in such circumstances with this condition who may complain that in twilight they can hardly see at all.

The spectacle wearers in ordinary schools as well as in schools for the blind and partially sighted will often be children whose vision is imperfect because of refractive errors as a result of an abnormal length or shape of the eyeball. The short-sighted or myopic child seems to have acquired a legendary aura of studiousness, perhaps because he can often see small detail in the near environment, and may thus have much less difficulty with tasks close to him, such as reading and fine drawing, than he has with those involving distance vision, for example when he is playing outdoor games. The eyeball in the case of the myopic child is excessively long causing blurring of focusing; in most cases it is possible to correct this by the provision of spectacles with concave lenses. However, there is among children an extreme form of this condition, difficult to correct and it may also be present along with other diseases or defects of the eye. Fine (1968) noted myopia as the second greatest cause of visual defect among children born between 1956–60 entering schools or classes for the partially sighted. Here again she noted a family history of myopia.

Some children suffer from visual defects whose presenting symptoms are readily visible to the parent or teacher; for instance, a squint or strabismus, which may affect one eye (monocular), or both eyes (binocular) is shown by the eye or eyes turning inwards or outwards in a non-alignment. Often the cause is due to muscular imbalance, and it is important that corrective treatment perhaps by means of surgery, should be undertaken at the right time, since in order to overcome the effect of double vision, the vision in one eye may be suppressed and in time this eye may lose its usefulness. It is quite usual to cover one eye whilst the child is waiting for surgery in order to avoid this occurring. The whole problem of treatment becomes more complex if the squint is only one aspect of visual handicap and occurs along with other disorders.

A disorder of ocular movement, evidenced as a to-and-fro oscillation which may be apparent in both eyes, can also be present and co-exist with other visual problems. This movement may be very quick or slow, and its effect on seeing is difficult to assess. There may be a hereditary tendency towards this condition which is known as nystagmus.

The albino child, with light skin and hair and pale colouring of the iris, is frequently readily recognizable, although Fine comments on the fact that in schools for the partially sighted she saw albino children with complete absence of pigment (including some children of dark-skinned parentage) as well as children with apparently normal pigmentation who are found to be albinotic after careful scrutiny of the retina. It can be helpful for some of these children to be prescribed spectacles with tinted lenses, since they tend to be photophobic and like to avoid strong light. Their special needs in this respect can point up the necessity for the teacher to understand the individual requirements of visually handicapped children. On a bright day an albino girl of about 7 years of age was seen keeping close to the walls in the school gymnasium in order to be in the shadow, rather than joining in the game that was taking place in a patch of brilliant sunlight in the middle of the room. Once again, a family history of this condition can often be noted.

The physical bases of lack of sight or diminished sight can be numerous since any part of the eye can be damaged by trauma or disease, or be abnormal in its form. The optic nerve may be damaged by pressure, as with a tumour, resulting in pressure within the eyeball causing partial or total atrophy. In such a case the child may be aware of a darkish blank space just where the sharpest central vision would normally be present. When a child with this condition tries to read print the effect may be to obscure part of the letters.

Vernon Smith (1971) contends that all too little data is available on the way in which visual stimulus is modified on its way to the visual cortex in the brain, and concludes that it is therefore not possible to tie up a close relationship between the presence of a specific disease or abnormality of the eye and the way in which a child uses his sight. However, it is evident that a lack of binocular vision will affect the child's ability to perceive visuo-spatial relationships and diminish the range-finding function of the eyes, whilst refractory errors can cause blurred vision with difficulty in discriminating some visual forms. Defects of the visual field may occur when either the periphery or the centre of the retina is diseased or damaged.

One interesting link between the manifestation of a specific disease and performance level has been the cause of discussion and speculation particularly in schools for the blind. Over the years, teachers had tended to comment on the fact that a number of their most able pupils were cases of retinoblastoma, a condition of malignancy affecting one or both eyes, involving treatment of a radical nature when the sufferer is still in infancy. Williams (1968) pursued a line of investigation confirming that children with this condition tended to have a higher than normal intelligence quotient.

Incidence of visual handicap among school-age children in the UK

Henderson (1974) notes the decrease of blind schoolchildren in England and Wales from about 2,700 in 1920 to about 1,100 in 1971, commenting on the fact that control of infectious diseases and improvement in ante-natal care contributed to this. He observes that between 1948 and 1955 there was a sudden but sharp increase in the number of blind babies, due to the fact that those born prematurely and who were of very low weight at birth in some cases developed fibrotic changes in the tissues of their eyes after receiving oxygen considered necessary to save their lives. The resultant condition of severe eye damage became known as retrolental fibroplasia. Henderson concludes that congenital or hereditory causes are now the main reasons for blindness in the case of children in the UK, and that often the primary cause of the condition may be unknown. Since all blind and partially sighted children are not registered, the statistics based on the Blind Register which became the official record of the number of blind persons in 1919 may err on the side of underestimating the total. Professor Arnold Sorsby and the Department of Health and Social Security have compiled reports giving details of the incidence of visual handicap in all registered persons since 1948.

Taylor (1975) confirms the observation made by Henderson with regard to the reduction of cases of blindness in children since the introduction of antibiotics which he claims halved the rate of blindness in children by 1948, but he notes the increase in blindness caused by retrolental fibroplasia as a peak in the registration of older children in 1958. His figures for 1974 indicate a total number of 2,151 blind children from 0 to 15 years of age. He observes a static ratio in the 5 to 15 age-group of children registered as partially sighted with a rise of nearly 50 per cent in the 0 to 4-year-old group in the years between 1957 and 1968. The Department of Health and Social Security Statistics for 1974 show the number of blind children, receiving tuition either at school or at home and between the ages of 5 and 15 years as a total of 1,733 whilst the estimated number of partially sighted children in the same age-group for that year totalled 2,388. In addition to these figures of children registered as blind or partially sighted, it must be noted that the peripatetic and advisory services are encountering children within the full range of visual handicaps in schools and classes of many kinds not primarily designated as special schools for the blind or partially sighted. In these circumstances it is particularly necessary that an understanding of the problems of children whose sight is impaired, or who do not see at all, should be carefully developed. Some of the questions posed with regard to how best to provide appropriate education for visually handicapped children arise because even among the handicapped these children form a minority group. One can encounter a child with defective sight working without apparent difficulty in an ordinary classroom, but one can also find a severely visually handicapped infant who is multiply handicapped in a subnormality unit.

Problems in the definition of blindness and partial sight

Henderson observes that few of the children considered to be blind are totally blind, since it is possible for many of them to distinguish light from darkness and even to have some guiding sight enabling them to be aware of objects visually; children with a visual acuity of less than 3/60 are often considered to be educationally blind, especially if the visual field is restricted. Whilst the criterion for determining whether children considered to be partially sighted as having such poor vision that they require education by special methods is not clearly defined, many of these children have a visual acuity of less than 6/60 and again limitations in the visual field, or the presence of nystagmus or albinism, may be taken into account.

The descriptive term 'visually handicapped' is being increasingly used for children, although the medical categories of 'blind' and 'partially sighted' are still current in assessment and subsequent educational placement. It can be useful to consider 'visual handicap' as an umbrella term covering both categories, and describing a continuum having at one end the situation of total blindness, followed by mere perception of light through to perception and recognition of objects in the near and distant environment, and finally embracing the level of impaired sight which demands a minimum adaptation in the presentation of learning materials. It is a term too wide to embody precise definition, but the individual differences in apparent visual efficiency which children with impaired sight may show in a classroom situation can make the label of 'blind' or 'partially sighted' seem over-restrictive. The way in which a child interprets what he sees, already a complex process, can be complicated further by the accumulation or by lack of visual memories; perceptual, cognitive and motivational factors may have a bearing on the use made of impaired or diminished vision. To refer to a child as 'blind' can give an impression of complete sightlessness, implying the need for specially designed learning materials drawing upon tactile and auditory presentation. However since the majority of pupils even in special educational provision for the blind possess some degree of sight, even if it is very little, specialized teaching methods now place increasing emphasis on the utilization of any remaining vision. Some special schools have attempted to give a more flexible description of their provision by stating that it is for children 'with little or no sight', rather than for 'blind' children. The range of visual competence in schools, units and special classes for the partially sighted again covers a wide range with some overlap into the 'blind' category. It is necessary to use the two medico-legal terms 'blind' and 'partially sighted' when describing educational provision and in tracing its development, but the broader term of 'visually handicapped' more realistically describes the condition of many children who are nominally in either category.

2   Parents and children

Recognition of the need for parent counselling

Successive resolutions drawn from internationally based conferences concerned with the education of the visually handicapped have stressed that if the blind baby's education is to become effective it should be started by the parents' education, and that the parents themselves have the right to expect expert education for their child and supportive services for him from an early age. These statements highlight an area of agreement common both to research findings and the everyday experience of teachers and social workers, with the necessity for such provision yet again emphasized in two major educational reports in Great Britain. Although using general terms of reference with regard to handicap, the Plowden Report (1967) requires that parent advisory services should be a sequel to the early and accurate diagnosis of disability in children, whilst the Vernon Report (1972) elaborates the specific needs of counselling services for parents whose children are visually handicapped. A basic aim in providing these specialized advisory services must surely be to help to diminish the anxiety and apprehension of parents, and to encourage them to provide an environment that encourages the independence and active curiosity of the young visually handicapped child.

A preoccupation with physical safety is indeed understandable and to some extent appropriate in those caring for young children who do not see well, or perhaps at all, but the answer lies in providing circumstances in which movement can be encouraged safely rather than in restricting activity. Anecdotal examples of extreme over-protection such as that of the blind child left in bed for hours with the radio blaring, or the partially sighted 6 year old, sound in wind and limb, but brought to school daily in a pushchair, are not unknown to teachers. These examples may be more memorable than general, but the harder evidence of research leads Parmelee (1966) to suggest that such parental protectiveness may make undue numbers of blind children unable to handle even excellent infant programmes when these are first presented. Lairy and Harrison-Novello (1973) relate performance closely to family attitudes in the case of blind pre-school children, finding encouragingly that in the case of a group of manifestly over-anxious parents not only were the mothers responsive to counselling which helped them to understand their attitudes, but a striking improvement in the performance levels of their children followed such counselling.

Parental demand for advisory services Because of lack of quantification in so sensitive an area, it may be easy to underestimate the number of parents who accommodate and come to terms with the misfortune of their child's impaired sight. Langdon (1970a) encouraged the parents to speak for themselves, describing their reactions to the discovery of visual handicap in their child, and indicating the areas in which they would have welcomed both information and help. Anxiety and uncertainty appeared to have been exacerbated if diagnosis of the handicap had been unduly delayed; inability to understand medical terminology and the implications of visual loss or impairment proved in some cases to be an additional cause of distress. There was substantial appreciation for the medical care that had been received but an expressed need in many cases to discuss present and predicted problems with a worker concerned and knowledgeable about the management of young visually handicapped children. Since the majority of the persons on the blind and partially sighted registers in Great Britain fall within the middle or old age-groups, parents may well not have encountered these handicaps among children until faced with the situation in the midst of their own family. The circuitous way in which information about available help was sought through neighbours, or even in a local shop, is cited by Langdon as a call to improve the communication between those who provide and those who receive appropriate services for the visually handicapped. Langdon's survey shows that gratuitous and sometimes inaccurate advice was sometimes given to parents by non-professionals, but it may also be the case that the emotional response to blindness in particular inhibits the relaxed and easy discussion about children and their needs that might normally take place between parents, friends and neighbours. A sharpened awareness of the specific areas in which advisory and counselling provision is needed has followed Langdon's evidence and the subsequent recommendations of the Vernon Report with varying attempts to meet the needs thus exposed.

Early mother–child relationships

The mother of a severely visually handicapped baby may well be subject to considerable physical and emotional strain; the early mother–child relationship may be in risk of being disturbed if handling of the child by his mother is minimized or precluded because of medical or organizational necessity in hospital. Later on, too, there may not be the eye contact and the smiling response to her presence which the mother would normally expect from her child. As he grows and develops the infant will need more time devoted to his management than would be anticipated for a non-handicapped child, if he is to be given the opportunities to participate in the daily activities of feeding, helping to dress himself and playing actively. It may be difficult to keep the balance of attention to the rest of the family, since holidays and leisure activities as well as daily demands on time may need modification or at least forethought. However, the consequence of affectionate acceptance of the child as he is may well be crucial in helping him to capitalize on subsequent educational and social opportunities; this appears to be particularly relevant to his later development if such secure acceptance has as its sequel the provision of a reasonably stimulating and interesting environment which encourages exploration and discovery. In addition to the somewhat generalized statement of Sommers (1944) that any ensuing educational programme is likely to be affected by the attitude of parents towards their visually handicapped child and his handicap, Gomulicki (1961) states more specifically in a comparative study of blind and sighted children that good achievement in performance areas in the case of some of the skill subjects may be linked to the parents' encouragement of early self-reliance. Norris, Spaulding and Brodie (1957) conclude that favourable opportunities, including security within the family and in the understanding of the child's special needs, are benign conditions in the absence of which there may be enduringly detrimental effects on both the educational success and the personality development of the visually handicapped child.

Pre-school development and early activities It is vital that the young visually handicapped child is encouraged to handle objects in active play, since his deficient sight makes it difficult for him to consolidate experience as a result of discovery. Tobin (1971a) underlines the implication of this aspect of the cognitive development of children who see little or nothing in his co-ordination of some of the conclusions drawn from internationally based research.

Studies cited by Tobin which have a particular relevance to the stages of pre-school learning for these children include that of Tillman (1967) which indicates a general lack of integration of educational experience, so that each fragment of knowledge gained is 'cast into a separate frame of reference'. Studies of conservation show that blind children explore their environment differently from the sighted, whilst Zweibelson and Borg (1967) stated that blind children make less use of abstract concepts than the sighted. These observations may imply that from early years there can be a need to structure the search techniques for children who cannot use sight as an effective channel for integrating information. In order to help the young visually handicapped child to forge appropriate informational links Kaplan (1966) suggests the implementation of a carefully graded infant teaching programme, whilst the significance of the timely direction of activities and guided discovery is suggested by Stephens (1972). This worker in referring to the importance of visual activity in the development of concepts in the young sighted child, stresses the deprivations of the young blind child in the development of his sensori-motor schemas. Here again there is emphasis on the need for action learning at an early stage, since verbal description may supplement but not replace felt experience. Such research conclusions are in line with the experience of teachers who may find that these children not only have difficulty in integrating information, but also in generalizing a situation, or grasping the implications of an object or event in its total context; the misconceptions which can arise from fragmented and unrelated discoveries are nicely illustrated in the comment of a young blind child who on hearing a cow bellow asked his teacher, 'Which horn did she blow?'

The common denominator of ordinary childhood activities may be the baseline from which many learning situations can be developed as the visually handicapped infant participates increasingly in the activities of daily living. Even against the background of individual differences in reaching developmental stages which one expects to encounter among children, for the visually handicapped the readiness to sit alone, to pull himself up and to walk may come relatively late; there is some evidence that the crawling stage may not take place at all. Wills's (1965) observations of blind nursery school children lead her to make the supposition that a child lacking a major sense such as vision would understand his world later and in a different way from a child with full sensory equipment.

The need to handle, fondle and talk to the visually handicapped baby is crucial; in the early days after birth, when his world is mouth-centred, the physical presence of the mother giving love as well as food should be experienced. The non-handicapped baby will probably begin to be aware of sounds and to focus his eyes at about a month old, and in the ensuing weeks begin to show the beginning of hand-eye co-ordination. The effect of lack of sight on the early development of the child with a congenital visual handicap is still imperfectly understood and Reynell and Zinkin (1975) stress the need to try to understand the ways in which such children learn and make sense of their world rather than attempting to compare them with the sighted child minus the visual component. There is still much to be discovered about the development of the child who has never had the co-ordinating sense of vision compared with the child who has later been deprived of this. In working on new procedures for the developmental assessment of young children with severe visual handicaps Reynell and Zinkin constructed a motor scale with an assessment of manipulation, locomotion and reflex function, and a mental scale indicating levels of social adaptation, sensori-motor understanding, exploration of the environment including response to sound and subsequent verbal understanding and expressive language.

Since many babies with a visual handicap may also suffer from some degree of physical or neurological impairment attention is given in these scales to estimating hand function and locomotion. Some actions such as the precise finger and thumb movement required to control and release objects may be improved by practice. The scales contain items of this kind to help the child forward in his sensori-motor development. It is not the intention of this scheme to pay attention primarily to comparison and standardization but rather to explore the areas of learning and development of individual children, and to plan a programme of help for parents to carry out at home as part of their everyday dealings with the child.

Familiarity with the developmental stages of non-handicapped infants together with observation of the behaviour of visually handicapped ones can lead to suggestions of some common-sense adaptations in structuring play and learning situations. For example, the baby who receives little or no stimulation through vision will need to have small objects, some preferably audible, such as rattles or small bells within his reach. At the normal stage of sitting up with support, at about thirteen weeks or so, the visual panorama increases for the sighted baby; with less stimulation to respond to, the visually handicapped baby will require gentle encouragement to do this, and will probably enjoy holding and moving safe but interesting small objects put into his hands. By the age of approximately six months when the sighted baby is sitting for much of his time and frequently amusing himself with manipulating objects, the visually handicapped baby will be in particular need of having a good variety of articles to taste, handle, bang and drop, and it must be remembered that the boundaries of his world will be to a greater extent than for the sighted, the boundaries of the extent of his own reach.

Like the sighted baby, he will need the support and security of a daily routine through weaning. Towards the end of the first year there may be attempts to move from shuffling and trying to pull himself up, and when his limbs are strong enough he can be helped and encouraged to stand with support. The unhandicapped one-year-old may well be starting to walk but not stand alone, while his increasing co-ordination may enable him to throw a ball and pick up small objects. One can but suppose that the visually handicapped youngster who has reached a comparable stage of physical and neurological development will have fewer incentives to perform such actions, and will need more adult intervention to ensure that he has toys and objects available and is encouraged to reach out and grasp, to explore and move about. He will in any case need companionship in play, and should be beginning to respond to words and voice tones. The careful use of an appropriate 'reward' system may help him to consolidate his present levels and encourage him in progressive activities. The extent to which an intervention programme for blind infants can be effective is described by Fraiberg, Smith and Adelson (1969) with emphasis on the adult's work as interpreter to the blind infant.

The second year of life should see the visually handicapped as well as the sighted infant increasingly participating in self-help skills such as toileting and feeding, but parental anxiety for the child to be considered acceptable must not force these issues. Meal times for him as well as for the sighted child can have some of the aspects of a game.

The pamphlets produced by the Royal National Institute for the Blind entitled *Children with Severe Visual Handicap* give some guidance for parents and others concerned with the management of such children. The adaptations and methods suggested are both practical and appropriate.

Over his second year the visually handicapped child like his sighted peer should be beginning to understand commands that he hears often, thus opening up possibilities for more complex games and activities; this is a stage when his increasing physical activity and co-ordination make it vital that he should not be left unduly long in the confining security of the cot or high-chair, nor simply allowed a space on the floor for play which has been completely cleared of furniture and interesting objects. A large play-pen can be useful for some but not all play times, and sharp edges and corners of furniture can be padded for safety.

Development of pre-school programmes

In North America a number of infant programmes have been developed for visually handicapped children. These seem to be characterized by a check list of graded tasks linked to developmental stages and to a tight programme of structured activities. Whilst there is undoubted value in clarifying objectives in this way, perhaps some caution needs to be exercised lest tension and anxiety be linked to expectation of evident achievement in such young children. There has been evidence in past years of the effect of lack of stimulus and activity amongst young blind children, but over-teaching must not supersede this. The experimental work undertaken by Davidson (1975) in Ontario shows sensitivity to these issues and strikes a balance between the introduction of a specific graded activity and simply encouragement of the young blind child to enjoy his infancy in his own way.

Nursery school provision and playgroups   The recommendations which the Vernon Report (1972) offers for the provision of three types of nursery education to be available for visually handicapped pre-school children are not easy to implement because of the relatively low incidence of visual handicap; the dilemma is that expert teaching support which takes cognizance of the implications of the absence or limitation of sight on the child's learning and social situation may not be readily and continuously found in the general nursery school setting. Apart from attending an ordinary nursery school, it is suggested that the visually handicapped youngster might be included in a special nursery group for handicapped children with a variety of disabilities, or at a special unit for blind and partially sighted infants. However, there are in Great Britain rather few nurseries for handicapped children, although an increasing number of play groups, some specifically for the visually handicapped, are becoming established either through the social services or through the educational advisers in Local Authorities. A number of schools for the blind and for the partially sighted take a few children of nursery age or have a small nursery group, and the Hampstead Child Therapy Clinic has a small day nursery for young blind children. The Sunshine Homes, under the auspices of the Royal National Institute for the Blind, provide residential nursery education and a period of assessment for young blind and partially sighted children, usually those with additional handicaps or with home problems; the children whose visual disabilities are due to non-accidental injury may well need the continuity of care and special expertise of such a setting, rather than the more generalized support and perhaps frequent change of staff more likely to be encountered in some local authority short-stay homes.

The question of nursery school provision may arise at the age of three or four years. Certainly the activities which will be helpful in establishing body awareness, directionality and spatial orientation may to some extent be carried out within a small group of nursery-aged children of mixed visual ability, but much individual attention will need to be given to the child with little or no sight. Lyndon and McGraw (1975) point out that activities which may help to establish and reinforce concepts of action space, body space and object space need to be introduced at the appropriate stage of the child's development, since there can be a danger that he may have passed the stage in his maturation at which he could most readily and effectively accept such learning. The appropriate stage for gross motor movement and the beginnings of body awareness and early orientation should take place before acceptance at infant school level, with opportunities to develop and practice essential skills on which the future good posture and effective mobility of the child are likely to depend; the blind or poorly sighted child should be able to participate in action games involving parts of the body, such as 'Simon says ...' and to use appropriate toys and furniture in games for orientational landmarks and indications of the position of his own body in relationship to objects and space. Chanting, singing and movement to mime may help to counteract the rigidity and tension so often encountered in the muscles of young blind children and increase confidence through enjoyable and purposeful movement which may, to some extent, mitigate the tendency to walk with the arms stretched out in front and the head drooping.

Ideally, the visually handicapped infant of 3 to 4 years of age should be able to have some benefit from the social opportunities of mixing with other children at a nursery or initially in a playgroup. It must be well-understood that even the opportunity for the blind or partially sighted child to handle and play with objects will in many cases leave him with less comprehension of their totality and their function than will be evident to the fully sighted infant playing alongside him. Indeed the blind child successfully and happily attending an ordinary nursery school is featured in a number of American studies, and in Great Britain, too, this concept appears to be increasingly acceptable. The opportunities for social interaction with sighted children are stressed, but there are problems which must be faced realistically; certainly the readiness of the child to take advantage of playing and learning alongside sighted infants must be gauged and the family's needs and capacity to support him in this venture must be carefully considered; finally the ethos of the receiving school, its pressures, and the attitudes of the head and staff towards the additional responsibility of accepting a visually handicapped child must be fully discussed. The visually handicapped child is likely to need more time and more individual attention than other children in the group, and even if there is willingness to give this, other demands may make it difficult to do so adequately.

Specialized teaching techniques and materials

Since the basic skills leading to competent mobility and orientation, to communication and to self-help and physical independence are being established in the nursery years, specific and appropriate teaching techniques are needed if the child is to participate in the group activities available to him in the nursery school. The infant who has some residual vision will need both skilled help and perhaps some adaptation of materials if he is to be encouraged to use this maximally. It is still possible that the adults who are concerned with both his education and home-life may fear that using his sight will cause it to deteriorate as if it were an expendable property. Barraga (1964) has made a remarkable breakthrough in showing how visual efficiency appears to be improved as a result of structured training; she stresses that such training is likely to be most effective if it is started at least by the time the child attends nursery school and is continued throughout this period. Clearly the visual acuity itself is not altered as a result of training but the possibility of an improvement in perceptual capacity and in the ability to pay attention to visual stimuli seems likely to be increased.

The extent to which the child with some vision will need differently presented materials and play activities from the child who is totally blind in the pre-school years warrants much further research. Certainly in either case the availability of toys and materials for play in the near environment is essential. Encouragement to locate and identify auditory clues, the connection of words with objects and actions, and the tactile exploration of objects will require more specific intervention for children who are totally blind, whereas the provision of bright, attractive and preferably moving toys should be ensured for the child who possesses even very low visual acuity. It is in any case extremely difficult to assess the amount of useful vision of a young child, but in addition to the specific activities of visual enhancement put forward by Barraga (1970) there are a number of play situations suggested by Marshall (1969b) particularly for the pre-school child with limited vision.

Learning through play and discovery should be taking place both in an individual and a small group situation. Hills (1974) offers practical suggestions in presenting play materials and in the skilled adaptation of circumstances for young visually handicapped children with concomitant handicaps, particularly the rubella children.

Pre-school advisory services

It has become the practice of some local education authorities in Great Britain to appoint an educational adviser or peripatetic teacher with a particular responsibility for visually handicapped children, possibly with a working base at a school for blind or partially sighted children. The brief for such workers is wide and may involve the oversight of visually handicapped pupils in educational provision primarily geared to the needs of the fully sighted, or the physically or mentally handicapped. The class teacher who has among her pupils a child who can see little or nothing will need sufficient advice and information from a trained and expert worker about educational methods and adaptations that take cognizance of the implications of visual handicap in the learning situation. Such diverse demands mean a heavy load of work and travel for the peripatetic teacher or adviser, perhaps leaving insufficient time for seeing parents and gaining a knowledge of the home environment of the pre-school blind or partially sighted child. Inter-disciplinary co-operation is essential between social, health and educational services if these needs are to be met adequately. Social workers, if they are trained and experienced in dealing with blind and partially sighted persons will have had more contact with the older age-groups and are unlikely to have the specific knowledge of child development which would give them confidence in structuring activities for pre-school children. Teachers, on the other hand, may not be skilled in the techniques of home visiting, and without a training in case work find it more difficult to size up a domestic situation and help the parent in the home situation. Clearly consultation and teamwork are needed here to ensure that the home is not over-visited or even that contrary advice is not given.

The RNIB has developed and extended the work of a team of educational advisers many of whom are widely experienced in dealing with pre-school visually handicapped children. Since there are still many areas in Great Britain lacking a local authority adviser for the visually handicapped, their work in advising and co-ordinating existing information is especially valuable. The parents of visually handicapped children may, as individuals or as a group, almost unwittingly adopt the role of advisers.

Work of parent groups

In the USA where a number of groups of parents of handicapped children have been formed over many years, Katz (1961) noted that the primary motives expressed in the groups related to participating action either in obtaining help for individual children, or in attempting to improve facilities, knowledge and research about handicap. Although such aims might be considered either as laudable or as an intrusion into the realms of professional expertise, Katz concludes that the effect of such group activity is largely positive since he found striking and wide agreement among parents as to its therapeutic nature. Seemingly it offered channels for socialization, support and specific services, some of which might be unobtainable by families acting as individual units. Strategic professional workers able to bring psychological or organizational expertise might be sought by the group as key members. It may be that the apparently emotional or even negative attitudes of some parent leaders would be challenging for professional workers to handle, but as Gutkind (1952) observes, it is surely essential for the recipients of guidance to be drawn into participation actively, and at all possible levels.

Parent groups may not only be a means of disseminating information about available services, but might also be a potential source of dedicated personnel who, with appropriate training, could help to implement counselling and pre-school services for visually handicapped children. Parents have the great advantage in this situation of having shared problems and experienced day-to-day difficulties in the practical management of young children, finding their own ways of helping them to enjoy their childhood. Whilst the objectives and sequences of specialized pre-school activities need to be clarified and advice on developmental stages and the implications of visual handicap understood, parents may themselves be able to offer a spontaneous and intuitive understanding of the child's needs that should not be spoiled. In Great Britain the Partially Sighted Society, founded in 1973, includes an active body of parents of visually handicapped children; the Society holds regional and national conferences and publishes its own journal; such an organization is likely to view current eductional provision for partially sighted children both appreciatively and critically, and has already recommended increased nursery provision for visually handicapped children. Among the facilities which parents of these children themselves have requested, the following requirements were listed: early advice and help for parents; early diagnosis and registration of visual handicap in the child; opportunities for advice on pre-school activities including visual stimulation; information about local play groups and parent groups; and, finally, genetic counselling.

In the requests of these parents we have echoed in lay terms many of the same themes previously referred to in official recommendations. With such unanimity at so many levels expressed by those professionally and those personally concerned with the welfare of young visually handicapped children, the means of implementing and extending the necessary services has developed from the increased co-operation of all who have the appropriate expertise and concern. For these young children there is still more that can be done.

3 The development of educational provision for blind and partially sighted children

Early institutions for the blind

Past years have seen the growth of highly specialized educational facilities for blind children in particular, and current pressures for the reappraisal of their educational situation cannot be fully understood without some consideration of the ways in which this provision has developed. Fortunately it is rather well documented, with records and reports of long-established schools spanning the years, even centuries, and yielding a socially and historically fascinating picture. A number of the present special schools for blind children are directly rooted in the voluntary organizations which co-operate with the state and local authorities in providing education for blind children. All the early schools and institutions concerned with the visually handicapped were nominally for the blind; recognition of the presence of partial or defective sight as a condition which might require adaptations to teaching materials or compensatory education was only made well into the present century; possibly the full impact of evident blindness may have been more emotionally stirring. Certainly, attempts to protect and manage the lives of those afflicted by it chimed in with the aims of a number of religious and philanthropic groups and individuals, so that sheltered provision for the blind grew in the eighteenth and burgeoned in the nineteenth century. An increasing number of institutions, so called Asylums and Schools of Industry for the Blind were established during these years, bearing against today's thinking some of the hallmarks of patronage and isolation from society. Closer examination reveals some surprises, however, since interwoven with the repetitive tasks and the rigid routines of these institutions there are glimpses of vigorous and pioneering educational ventures, remarkable for their day. The Royal Normal College for the Blind (now named The Royal National College for the Blind) was founded in 1872 by

Armitage and Campbell, two blind men who seemed determined to prove that the blind could be active and independent. Photographs taken in the late nineteenth century of their blind students show them roller skating, fencing and riding articulated bicycles made for twelve; activities unavailable to many sighted adolescents of the day. By this time they were already training blind students to be teachers and piano-tuners and, before long, blind women as well as men left the College to earn their own living as typists and shorthand writers; education and training as well as occupation were becoming realities for some of these young blind people at least. Already the scene had changed since the founding in 1791 of the School for the Blind in Liverpool by Edward Rushton, a man himself blinded as a result of infection caught from slaves on board ship, whilst Blair had established Worcester College in 1866 for the blind sons of gentlemen. The development of educational provision for the blind is ably described by Pritchard (1963).

The Education Act of 1893 made it the duty of local authorities to ensure that blind and deaf children had educational opportunities. Indeed, in this Act blind children were to receive schooling from the age of 5 to 16 years, although at the time the normal age for leaving school was 12 years of age.

The Royal National Institute for the Blind In 1868 a voluntary organization was inaugurated by Armitage which in time became the Royal National Institute for the Blind; this voluntary body today sponsors some of the well-known schools for the blind in Great Britain, including a selective school for girls and schools for multiply handicapped blind children. It supplies specialized apparatus and braille books and has developed supportive advisory and educational services on a national scale.

Special schools for blind and partially sighted children

Throughout the nineteenth century when many of them were founded, and into the twentieth century, the special schools for the blind have provided the nucleus of education for the majority of blind children in Great Britain. By now most of the schools are co-educational and cater for the full age range from 5 to 16 years

31

at least. Basically residential schools, their pattern has been increasingly one of weekly boarding, or at least frequent week-end visits home by pupils. Greater flexibility within these schools often includes provision for daily pupils who live within reasonable travelling distance and varying degrees of co-operation and, in a few cases, partial integration with neighbouring schools for the sighted. These schools are subject to the inspectorate, and are staffed by fully qualified teachers who must also hold additional specialized qualifications to teach the blind; the numbers in each school are small, seldom being more than 150 pupils, and class groups are not usually composed of more than twelve pupils so that there is an emphasis on meeting the needs of the children on an individual basis. The Education Act of 1944 laid on local authorities the obligation to provide education appropriate to the 'age, ability and aptitude' of the pupil. In the case of the blind pupil the appropriate education has been frequently considered to be that of a residential special school for the blind, and the local authority pays the fees of the blind child to the administering body of the school. Because of the historical basis of the growth of education for the blind, some regions of the country (notably Cumbria, East Anglia, and Hampshire/Isle of Wight) do not have a school for the blind in their midst and some areas in the North of England (e.g. Newcastle) have schools for blind children of primary school age only. It will be readily seen that one of the problems facing those planning and administering the education of blind children in the UK is to use resources as effectively as possible in the face of the reality of the small and widely scattered school-age population of blind children.

Special nursery schools for blind children   Residential nursery schools for blind children between the ages of 2 and 7 years are maintained by the Royal National Institute for the Blind. Much has changed since these 'Sunshine Homes', as they were originally called, were founded in 1918 for blind babies. Now each home caters for a small number of children, seldom more than twenty, offering a period of residential assessment as well as nursery schooling for young visually handicapped children with clearly defined needs such as heavy additional handicaps or pressing social reasons for residential care and early education, and the designation has been altered to Sunshine House Nursery Schools.

Past years had their toll of blindness in young children as a result of infection and even malnutrition, but contemporary problems necessitating specialized help for very young children include those of blindness resulting from baby battering (Zadik, 1973).

Special schools and units for partially sighted children As would be expected from the higher incidence of partial sightedness, there are in the UK many more schools and units for children considered to be partially sighted than for children considered to be blind. However, fewer of these schools are administered by voluntary bodies. Although there are some residential schools, there is more opportunity for partially sighted children to attend special day schools or units, and an increasing number of these schools are accepting and making some provision for pupils who are on the blind register. Small groupings are again the case, seldom with more than fifteen pupils in a class. The specialized aspects of the schools and units are evident in the adaptations to the teaching environment, in the lighting, furniture, in the use of optical aids and in some instances enlarged print and diagrammatic material. Closed circuit television, audio–visual aids and other adaptations in the presentation of material are used in the teaching situation. Two residential schools have remained over the years as providers of educational facilities for both blind and partially sighted children in the same setting.

Changing attitudes towards the education of the visually handicapped

It was the Regulations following the 1944 Education Act which effectively differentiated the education of the partially sighted child from that of the blind child, although a case had been made for differences in the teaching approach and presentation of materials by some educators as early as 1902. By 1908 the first special school in the world for partially sighted children, usually referred to at this time as myopes, was opened in London for fifteen pupils. At that time and for many years afterwards, although the fact that such children possessed sight was recognized, they were heavily discouraged from making active use of it. Lightfoot (1948) describes the short working time and the frequent 'rest' periods that these children had to undergo. They even entered their school through a door bearing the inscription 'Reading and Writing shall not enter here'. The fear that visual activity might exacerbate faulty eye conditions was one of the few bonds at this time between educators of the blind and the partially sighted. In schools for the blind in the earlier part of the century, children with any residual vision were discouraged from peering at braille dots to help their groping fingers in deciphering the configurations; it was even known for paper bags to be put on their heads to render such 'cheating' impossible, whilst the few partially sighted children in schools designated for them, endured 'sight saving' methods which must have limited their curriculum and their adventurousness.

However, the newly formed schools for the partially sighted after 1944 had a more robust approach and emphasis on the visual presentation of learning material was made. It was at last realized that in general terms a child would be unlikely to damage his eyes by using them for work. Brightly coloured pictures were put on classroom walls; children were helped and encouraged to paint, to read print, to watch films. Attention was given to windows, to lighting, and to the position of desks. Partially sighted children ceased to be discouraged from holding their books close to their noses in order to see the print better. Instead of discouragement they were given reading stands and desks with slanting tops so that they could choose a reading and working position that was close to the eye but comfortable. The range of school subjects increased, although a limiting fear remained that some children might develop detached retinas if they undertook vigorous physical activities. It has also increasingly become the policy in schools for the blind to give more positive encouragement and realistic opportunities to pupils to use any residual vision that they may possess in their school work, and in their social environment.

Diversity of educational provision for visually handicapped children

Units for partially sighted children are sometimes attached to schools for the sighted, providing varying degrees of integration in the work and activities of the mainstream school. Local authorities in some areas have set up a peripatetic teaching service giving specialized help to individuals or small groups of partially sighted children both in mainstream education and in schools for children with other handicaps. These services can range from a co-ordinated team of teachers in one area, to a single adviser who travels wide distances giving help to non-specialist teachers in the adaptation of materials and in the understanding of the learning problems of any partially sighted children who may be in their classes.

Thus it will be seen that across the whole group of visually handicapped pupils, blind and partially sighted, there is theoretically a variety of types of educational placement. For the blind child there is the residential special school, increasingly with the opportunity for weekly boarding, or day attendance if the travelling distance from home makes this feasible; for the partially sighted child there is the day or residential school, again with weekly attendance, and the residential provision in a few schools for children in both the blind and partially sighted categories.

The partially sighted child may attend a special day school or a unit which adjoins a school for fully sighted children. In this situation there may be varying degrees of integration into the classwork and activities of the main school. A comparable situation exists for a few blind children who attend some or all of the classes in schools for the sighted near to the school for the blind, which supplies resource teachers to help the children and advise the teachers in the sighted school, also undertaking responsibility for the adaptation of materials, the production of braille and tactile diagrammatic work. A visually handicapped child, more likely to be deemed partially sighted than blind, may attend an ordinary school with regular help from a peripatetic teacher or adviser and have some adaptations to furniture and equipment, use of optical aids and magnifiers to help facilitate his work. Situations in which the visually handicapped pupil is in mainstream provision with some specialized help and appropriate modifications of equipment and learning materials appear, at first sight, to be particularly inviting since they offer the advantages of broader social contacts than those offered by the special school or even unit, but also attempt to provide the specialized methods needed to mitigate the effect of visual handicap in the learning situation. However, problems can arise if the specialized help is insufficiently frequent or the adviser insufficiently expert not only in the adaptation of materials but in understanding the implications of visual handicap. It is not enough for a child to be able to 'manage' in a given set of circumstances; he needs to have the help and, if necessary, specialized circumstances to enable him to reach his optimum potential. Because their sight defect is barely noticed some visually handicapped children are 'accidentally' integrated into educational provision not primarily designed for their needs. They may even be both successful and happy as a result of this, but school failure and a sense of personal failure could be the sequel to an imperfect or even total lack of understanding of their problem by teachers and other pupils.

The visually handicapped pupil in the ordinary school

Preparation for placement   The peripatetic adviser or teacher can do much to help in the successful placement of visually handicapped pupils in an integrated situation. By making arrangements for pre-school activities, possibly involving play-groups or nursery attendance, the first steps in group activities with fully sighted children will be taken. All arrangements for the acceptance of the child in his first school should be made well in advance, including a visit by the parents, and a realistic consideration of transport arrangements should be made. In order to suggest suitable placement, the peripatetic teacher must know the special and the regular schools in the area well, and must also keep under continuous review the progress and social adjustment of the visually handicapped child.

Supportive services   Teachers who have not had specialist training in visual handicap will need advice on the management of this and may have questions about eye conditions as well as about the presentation of materials and the adaptation of the environment. The adviser must be ready to listen and to observe so that the guidance he offers meets the need of the pupil and his teacher whose confidence and trust he must foster. It is important that information recorded from both assessment and observation of the child in an integrated setting should be clear and acceptable to the different professionals involved in the educational placement of such a pupil.

The amount of supportive help that individual children will

need from the peripatetic services will vary considerably. There will be some children with a minimal handicap who are quite rightly placed in ordinary schools, especially if they show a good level of social adjustment. Such children may have been provided with low vision aids which are helpful in school work. Children functioning successfully in this way may be regarded as 'contact' cases for the peripatetic services; minor adaptations to lighting or work position may help them but any unexpected failures should not be ignored.

Some visually handicapped children will require frequent and regular help, and much more radical adaptations in their learning materials – possibly with extended time in performing some of their school tasks. In order to supply appropriate diagrams, braille copies, or tactile material, the peripatetic teacher needs a base, either in the form of a special school for the blind or the partially sighted, a special unit or, at the least, a resource room. The support needs of children with differing handicaps present a variety of challenges in terms of the provision of resources. For children with a severe visual handicap learning material tends to be bulky and rather expensive. It can be quite a task to produce enough quickly made current and expendable tactile learning material. Voluntary transcribers, including serving prisoners, have done a great deal of work in helping to meet this need. It must be remembered that special codes in braille are used in the transcription of foreign languages and mathematics and that special equipment is also used in mathematics. Sister Clare (1965) stresses that when books are prepared for use by blind pupils in an ordinary school the text must be exact, and arranged so that the pupil can find the place easily, with small volumes and sighted page numbers given. It is also important that any specially prepared material is ready before and not after parallel work has been presented in class, and this can only be the case if planning has been a matter of co-operation between the regular and the peripatetic teacher. Areas in which the severely visually handicapped pupil will be likely to need specialized help include communication skills, physical independence including self-help skills and mobility. His teacher may need guidance with regard to lighting, the pupil's working position, any necessary adaptations to the curriculum, the care and effective use of any optical aids, individual presentation of material, including replications of blackboard work. Any social or psychological consequences of visual handicap must not be overlooked. The suitability of the leavers' programme and recommendations relating to further education and vocational or occupational placement will need consideration by the specialist and the regular teacher, as well as the careers officer. It may also be helpful for contact to be made and maintained with the social services.

Three types of integration In considering that the integration or the segregation of handicapped pupils is a false alternative, the Joint Council for the Education of Handicapped Children (1975) underlines the fact that it is not easy for peripatetic staff to provide expertise across a wide range of handicaps, nor to act as resource teachers for the whole range of secondary education, nor yet to guarantee sufficient and appropriately timed service for all the children in an area who need it. The necessity for planning in terms of man-power and resources rather than engaging in vigorous but often simplistic argument on the issue of integration of handicapped children (including the visually handicapped) is thus underlined. Such planning must involve a consideration of staff/pupil ratio, the availability of special apparatus and equipment, and the provision of supportive services, possibly on a team basis to a much greater extent than is at present generally the case. The question of special qualifications for teachers also requires examination, since it is a somewhat anomalous situation for a teacher in a special school for the blind to have to obtain special qualification within three years of appointment whilst a peripatetic worker, who is a source of advice on visual handicap for teachers as well as children, is not under the same obligation.

The support of peripatetic services does not provide the only way by which visually handicapped pupils may be integrated into schools for the sighted. An ultimate aim might be that all schools should be 'special' in providing a high staff/pupil ratio, carrying a number of people with special qualifications on the staff, and having a well-lit, well-planned environment in which further special adaptations for the visually handicapped could be easily incorporated. The human element embodied in the acceptance of the child as he is, by pupils and staff, is a further essential feature. A mid-way solution between the idealistic open form of education and the special school is the special unit attached to an ordinary school. Some of the problems here may result from a wide range of ages among the children in the unit as well as a considerable span in terms of ability and of visual competence. The positive advantages include the fact that the child may be able to live at home, but the relationship of the unit staff and children to the main school must be an accepting and highly co-operative one if the advantage of the unit situation is to be real rather than nominal.

There have been some successful examples of the special school being used as a home base, not only for peripatetic services, but also in cases where, for example, a near-by comprehensive school makes it possible for a number of secondary pupils to undertake most, or at least some, of their work alongside sighted pupils, but with the specialist support of the staff at the base school. One of the problems here, is that a good deal of time can be used in travelling between the base and the comprehensive school, but the wider range of curriculum in the school for the sighted may mean that on balance there is benefit to the pupil. The staffing at the base special school in such a scheme must allow for a close liaison with the staff of the comprehensive school and the complementary roles of both will need to be recognized. Although there is some risk that the visually handicapped child may find his identity, as well as his time, divided in such a system it does extend the work of the special school and provides the staff of the ordinary school with expert advice from those experienced in the teaching of visually handicapped children.

The multiply handicapped child with a visual handicap

Children with a visual handicap and communication difficulties The combination of visual defect with physical disability, such as spasticity; with hearing loss or impairment, as in the case of some children affected by rubella; with mental subnormality or retardation, presents a complex task to the educator. So complex indeed that it demands more detailed study and analysis than can be encompassed in a work of this nature, although the points made with regard to mobility and self-help skills, learning through listening, discovery by touch, and the enhancement of residual vision will have some relevance in the education of children whose multiple handicaps include visual defect.

39

A crucial area likely to be affected by the combination of defects is that of communication, without which the child cannot progress socially and intellectually. The problems of the deaf–blind child in this regard are obviously severe, and for these children the transmission and reception, not only of information, but of emotion and intention, must be developed through multi-sensory communication and response. Without speech the visually handicapped child has lost much of his communication with society, but gestures may be a viable means of supplementing or to some extent replacing this. Language disorder may be the result of a deficiency either in the inner or the oral language, due to delayed development, physical causes including local abnormalities or disorders or those of the central nervous system which combined with severe visual impairment, can result in a considerable limitation in the child's ability to communicate.

Sub-normal visually handicapped children Children affected by the rubella syndrome carry a particular risk of a combination of defects including sight and hearing defect, and Tobin et al, (1972) undertook studies in the subnormality unit in a hospital where, among the thirty children encountered, a large proportion were rubella cases. The observer was struck by the apparent passivity of the children, except in the case of a few who were hyper-active, and he felt that the paucity of their physical, social, and psychological experience was evident in the restricted range of their activities. To increase exploration he recommended the provision of toys with varied and complex shapes, since some of the bigger toys such as rockers, hoppers, and tricycles, appeared to encourage repetitive fixated behaviour. He also suggested that the training of these children should have a Piagetian basis which tries to build up manipulation, joining, matching and intention, and progresses through repetition, repetition with variation, finally achieving symbolic behaviour. In studying the effect of operant conditioning with these children the results were inconclusive, except in the case of vocalization where one child showed dramatic improvement. In order to maximize the effect of this approach to training, it is stressed that each child needs to have his own rewards and reinforcers identified, and that the goals must be specified in relation to existing levels of functioning. With regard to the utilization of staff time in such programmes, attempts should be made to develop some automatic 'teaching machines' in the form of tape recorders and toys to absorb some of the tedious reinforcement schedules, but it is also vital that all new staff should be trained in the principles and methods of conditioning.

Whilst there is inevitably some debate regarding the ethics and efficiency of conditioning, the urgency of developing viable schemes of training for severely retarded visually handicapped children is irrefutable. Simon and Leary (1972) in the same study draw attention to the incidence of severe mental retardation in the 0 to 4 age-group as being in the region of 73 per 100,000 of the population; of those in hospital at that date 1 in 5 had defects of hearing or vision, whilst 1 in 20 were blind. The children observed in this study had been rejected from provision by education authorities but developments since the date of this study have emphasized education, not simply care, as being the right of severely mentally, as well as physically, handicapped children.

Educational provision for multiply handicapped visually impaired children Existing educational provision for visually handicapped children with multiple defects includes the Ellen Terry Home at Carshalton for blind mentally retarded children, the Sunshine House Nursery Schools and two special schools sponsored by the RNIB. Of these, Rushton Hall in Kettering accepts pupils in the 8 to 12 age-group whilst Condover Hall in Shropshire caters for the 12 to 17-year-old pupils but has a unit for the deaf–blind known as Pathways for deaf–blind pupils from 5 to 17 years of age. A unit for multiply handicapped blind pupils of the full educational age-range is attached to the Royal Victoria School at Newcastle upon Tyne.

It is not only the training provided but the whole ethos of the school that needs to be both positive and caring for such severely handicapped children. An interdisciplinary approach by the staff is essential if the school is to become a meaningful community in which there is a humane acceptance of the children. This view is crystalized in the account by Myers (1975) of the way in which Condover Hall School developed. From the first, emphasis was placed on social development with a family unit system providing the pattern in residential accommodation. Attention has also consistently been given to encouraging physical independence and individual lessons in mobility are given as well as group activities, including camping, boating, and archery, offering the challenge of adventurous pursuits, even to the severely handicapped.

There is a pressing need to develop educational programmes for visually handicapped children who are in schools and units for the deaf, the educationally subnormal, and the physically handicapped.

What should they learn? Questions of curriculum content will arise in the case of multiply handicapped children with the likelihood of considerable emphasis being placed on the development of skills concerned with efficient living and with recreational activities. Bonham (1967) described her work with very retarded blind children, most of whom were illiterate. She found that they could be successfully involved in centre of interest programmes embodying practical work in the classroom, and in educational visits to places of interest, with emphasis being placed on the use of language with a practical, meaningful basis. To further the interest in language she gave time to poems and stories relating to the central theme undertaken and also involved the children in arranging, as well as in participating, in the visits. She stressed that her approach was not new, simply effective. Such a scheme gives life to the six basic educational areas widely considered as being fundamental for multiply handicapped children with visual defects, covering self-help skills (including feeding, dressing and grooming), social skills (self-control, group participation, etc.), independent-living skills (looking after one's own belongings, mobility), language skills (auditory, oral, articulation) and academic skills where these are appropriate. Within the framework of such planning, opportunities must be provided for the extension of the exploration that enables the child to gain a knowledge of size, shape, and distance. A combination of perceptual retardation co-existing with visual handicap demands a good deal of individual or small group work with the teacher. Free play is essential but does not always provide sufficient direction in the acquisition of sensory experience, so that this must be presented in a form of graded complexity. Francis-Williams (1966) describes learning situations of this type in work with children with minimal brain dysfunction who gradually learn differences between things that are of contrasting texture, temperature, and density and then relate the relative position of objects in space. Step-by-step discoveries of this kind are even more necessary for the child who sees little or nothing, and if such a child is also distractible or has a short attention span he will need a quiet and unstimulating background with activities ready for his moments of concentration.

Children who are emotionally disturbed   Emotional maladjustment can be a high risk in the case of a child who is visually handicapped, and Fine (1968) encountered a considerable amount of this in the blind and partially sighted children in her survey. She did not define the term and based her conclusion on teacher ratings; since some of the teachers questioned may have been unused to the responses of visually handicapped children the extent of maladjustment among these pupils may possibly be over-stated. However, Williams (1969) refers to the incidence of psychiatric disorder in blind children as being more than twice that of the normal child population, also stating that children with disabilities of the central nervous system are more than five times as likely as normal children to suffer such disturbances. He nevertheless claims with justice that since over two-thirds of the children with organic conditions affecting the central nervous system do not suffer from psychiatric disorders, there is support for the view that even severe disorders can be compatible with good adjustment. Even cases of damage to the brain with the sequel of a diminished capacity for adjustment and learning need not be incompatible with good emotional adjustment. He concludes that environmental stress in infancy and early childhood is likely to be an underlying cause of disturbed behaviour and the likelihood of this is increased yet again if the child is both premature and blind. But he makes the firm statement that the quality of maternal handling and of the early environment is of greater significance than birth weight, complications of pregnancy, or blindness in the subsequent development of personality and in the aetiology of behaviour disorders. In 1969 the Mary Sheridan Unit was opened under his direction for the study and both short and long-term treatment of visually handicapped children with severe personality and behaviour disorders.

The positive philosophy directing the work of this unit is that even the severely incapacitated blind child is capable of some socially acceptable responses and may need opportunities to develop his potential, while the factors which cause stress must both be identified and alleviated. It is the aim in the treatment of the child's psychiatric disorder eventually to enable him to return to the school from which he came or to proceed to another school. The basic objective of the multi-disciplinary team directing the unit is described by Argles (1971) as working to understand one another's views and methods, to contribute individually to decision making, to act co-operatively upon one another's decisions, to explain the objectives to new members and to explain team-work to others. In helping children with conduct disorders to attain a more controlled personality, the aim is to provide satisfactory alternatives to destructiveness. Praise and appreciation of efforts in self-control is marked, whilst necessary sanctions are applied swiftly and consistently.

Children with low vision and limited vision

An attempt to give a finer definition to terminology has been undertaken by Barraga (1976) in her clear description of children as blind if they possess only light perception without projection; as 'low vision' if they have limitations in distance vision, but are able to see objects and materials in the near environment within a few inches or at most a few feet; these children, she stresses, can in most cases use their low vision for school learning activities, including print reading, but are likely to need specialized help and encouragement to do so; finally Barraga describes as 'visually limited' those children who *are* in some way limited in the use of their vision in normal circumstances. Perhaps they will need special lighting or be helped by prescriptive lenses or use optical aids; they are children who see imperfectly, but should be considered as seeing children.

Barraga thus effectively puts a third category between the blind and visually limited (or partially sighted child as the description would be in the UK). Her intermediate category of low-vision describes aptly some of the children who may be encountered in special schools and educational provision for both the blind and the partially sighted. It is a corner stone of Barraga's educational philosophy that any assessment of vision should be thus closely defined and have as a sequel to definition appropriate intervention and educational placement. She has emphasized over many years of teaching and research that perceptual, motivational and cognitive factors play a considerable part in the eventual effectiveness of the child's visual efficiency; a statement of measured visual acuity is not a sufficient guide for educational purposes, and to this end her Visual Efficiency Scale (1970) seeks to indicate the actual, present level of the child's seeing in functional terms.

Nevertheless the information yielded from medical records about the cause and extent of the child's visual defect needs to be considered by the teacher in its implication for the day-to-day tasks which the child will undertake at school. If he has some sight, but too little to perform ordinary school work without adaptations and the need for specialized help, he will rightly be considered as 'having limited vision'. In practice, such children are likely to be considered as among the better seeing in schools for the blind, and amongst the most severely visually handicapped in schools for the partially sighted.

In a normal classroom and without special aids, writing on the blackboard could appear mere scribble to a child with low vision if he could see it at all even from a front desk, and visual aids shown by the teacher to the class as a whole may be indistinguishable to him. A lot of the small day-to-day tasks accomplished quite easily by other children can present him with a good deal of difficulty; cutting out shapes or cutting along a marked line with scissors is a difficult feat for a child with low vision; pouring liquid from a test tube in a science lesson, or measuring quantities of dry ingredients in cookery are likely to present difficulties, and it is a particular hindrance in his learning that he may not be able to copy a process demonstrated by the teacher, whether it be hooking wool through canvas or simply forming a letter, because he cannot see clearly the fine movements involved in these actions. Writing can be a particularly hard task because of visuo-motor problems; an inability to see where to start the formation of a letter and how to continue to draw its shape leads some children to try to work out for themselves with difficulty, sometimes inappropriately, the way in which a letter is formed. As a child with low vision progresses into secondary school there can

45

be new as well as continuing problems; the print size in books is likely to be smaller than in the case of primary school readers, and even more finely printed information may be presented to him in the form of tables, graphs and footnotes. Illustrative information becomes increasingly complex, and he may need to consult reference books and encyclopedias containing minuscule photographs and diagrams.

School achievement in visually limited pupils   The individual differences in the effect of visual impairment among children with limited vision are great, and so it is hardly surprising that research on the achievement and adjustment of children with poor sight often renders conflicting evidence. Lansdown (1969) draws attention to the range of opinions held even by teachers of the partially sighted. In recent years attention has been focused on the particular problems of children in this 'no-man's land' between blindness and sight, hardening into two main lines of attack on their learning problems. One stems from the medical and technical advances, the other from psychological and educational ones; together they offer the prospect of ameliorating the daily work and play situation for many children with low vision.

Low vision aids   Not all children with defective vision are suited to or can benefit from low vision aids, but they have been successfully prescribed and used in increasing numbers (Silver and Gould 1976); the aids may be in the form of spectacle-mounted telescopic lenses for distance vision or microscopic lenses for close work. It is this development that provides considerably greater degrees of magnification, for instance, than is possible with the single lens of the conventional spectacle, and which in some instances means that a child previously needing to use braille for reading can move on to using ink-print as a reading medium, since the low vision aids are sometimes helpful in cases of much lower vision than those amenable to correction by other means. The telescopic aid, since it is often used for such activities as watching sport or checking a street name, can be provided as a hand-held monocular accessory; for classroom work, distance vision tasks such as reading the blackboard or interpreting wall-mounted illustrative material, activities previously referred to as difficult or impossible for the unaided low-vision child, can in some cases be considerably facilitated by using spectacle-mounted telescopic aids. These can be made more useful for classroom use by being fitted with reading caps so that they need not be constantly removed when the pupil changes to near vision tasks such as reading or drawing. For near vision tasks, however, a microscopic aid based on the principle of two separated lenses can afford high levels of magnification. The visual field is inevitably much reduced and work must be held close to the lens in order to be discriminated.

Magnification Less sophisticated forms of magnification can be useful for some visually handicapped children; indeed a form of magnification is effected with no optical aids at all simply by bringing reading material closer to the eyes; in most cases the flexible character of the lens accommodates to the close distance without difficulty and a visually handicapped child will often spontaneously bring his working materials close to his gaze; the points for the teacher to watch here are to see if the working position can be made easier and more comfortable when holding the work at a near distance does seem helpful to the pupil. The work must be placed in a position where the reader does not have to bend over it, cramping his posture and probably casting a shadow on to the page; the range of one to four inches away from the eyes may seem a disquietingly close one to teachers unused to children with impaired vision, and adaptations to classroom furniture as described below may need to be considered.

Magnifiers are available in the form of strong convex lenses similar to those worn by people who have had the lens of the eye removed as a result of cataract operation, thus needing a substitute for its refractive function. Spectacles can be a form of magnifier with unifocal, bifocal or trifocal lenses providing the exact correction required for the specific eye defect; as with low vision aids, the child will sometimes need persuasion to wear them, with care that this does not become an emotional issue; in time the ability to see better can itself be the best form of persuasion as when a youngster tried to insist on wearing his glasses in bed in order to see his dreams better! The lenses of low vision aids, spectacles and magnifiers, must be kept clean and unscratched, and preferably kept in cases when not in use. They should not be laid down with the lens surface on the tops of desks or tables which may have dust and grit on them. Contact lenses having a comparable correction to spectacle lenses, can be used for some defective sight conditions and have the advantage of being virtually undetectable.

Non-prescriptive magnifiers are available in a number of different sizes and shapes, with a variety of frames, either to stand over the material to be viewed or to be hand-held, head-mounted or worn as a pendant. The lenses mounted in a circular or oblong frame with a handle are useful for examining print or small diagrams and objects for a short time; they have the advantage of being easy to position at the right distance and angle for scrutinizing material closely, but would be tiring to use for longer periods of reading when a stand magnifier would better serve the purpose. Some stand magnifiers are mounted on a plastic bridge shaped frame; there is a long oblong-framed magnifier known as the 'directory' magnifier which fits over a line of print, but probably one of the most useful is the small circular magnifier sometimes known as the 'cataract' lens. Lenses with a power of 5X and 8X can be useful for some visually handicapped children, and the addition of self-contained illumination from battery power seems to increase the effectiveness in a few conditions. The higher the power of the magnifier the smaller will be the area enlarged, with the result that in reading print only very short words or parts of words will be visible at one time and diagrams and illustrations will be fragmented. There is the problem, too, of peripheral distortion in some of the larger magnifiers. Some specialized adaptations such as the 'Nature Viewer', which is composed of a screw-topped plastic container permit the examination of small botanical specimens and insects.

The teacher's point of view about the use of magnifiers is likely to be communicated to the child. It takes time and trouble to try out the various forms of magnifiers and find one that best suits both the particular child and the particular purpose; finding the best distance from eye to magnifier and magnifier to material, ensuring that illumination is good but not dazzling, is yet another task for the teacher to undertake; magnifiers will not be helpful in all cases and in all circumstances, and where they are it may be better to make quite sure that a prescribed low vision aid could not be even more effective. However, they can provide a simple, portable and useful means of helping some visually handicapped children in using their vision more easily.

Training children to use vision effectively Whilst considerable advances have been made in the provision of individually prescribed low vision aids and various forms of magnifiers, there have been no less dynamic advances in exploring the processes of visual perception and harnessing this increased understanding for the use of children with visual impairments, by developing graded schemes and materials that lead from simple tasks to those of a complex perceptual visual nature.

As a basis it is necessary to assess the way the child uses his vision in functional terms and then lead him to a structured programme of standardized material that can help him to make maximum use of it; for whilst it is the sphere of medical and technical expertize to diagnose and treat a condition if it is amenable to treatment, and to prescribe individual glasses or low-vision aids and advise on their use, it must be the teacher's aim to ensure that the child has appropriate material to look at, to provide a suitable progression of complexity and size of work, and because of his daily interaction with the child give him the encouragement and motivation to enjoy trying to see, and to interpret what he sees, with or without an aid.

Visual enhancement programmes in the USA The child needs to learn to use his sight however impaired it may be before he is provided with a low vision aid, so that he has paid some attention to visual stimuli through using his own natural visual equipment before trying to use a low-vision aid or magnifier.

This is a point of view underlying the work of Barraga (1974) whose work in the USA during the 1960s bears the conviction that visually handicapped children, especially those described as blind, but in fact with some vision, may be in possession of an under-used capacity for seeing. She claimed that the measurement of visual acuity had been used too often and in too definitive a way as a guide to educational placement, resulting sometimes in the use of braille as a communication medium for children who were legally, but not, she considered, in the true sense educationally blind. Instead of early and restrictive classification, she recommends a short-term intensive teaching procedure that may improve the visual efficiency of low-vision children and indicate the most appropriate educational approach to be followed for them.

Her initial study (1964) set out to determine whether the visual behaviour of legally blind children with low vision could be improved by an intensive period of instruction based on a progression of enlarged and adapted educational materials. The subjects chosen were children whose levels of residual vision were extremely low and who had received no specific instruction in the visual discrimination and recognition of learning materials. In fact they had all previously used tactile and auditory materials in the classroom; they were children not known to have any additional abnormalities, and they were pupils attending a residential school for the blind. In what is described as 'an enriching programme of visual stimulation' the children taking part in the study were given a carefully graded programme using visually presented materials; the progression extended through geometric forms and outlines for visual discrimination, with single simple and then increasingly complex objects to look at and recognize, through the pictures and finally letters and words in print. It is emphasized that the composition of the graded lessons reflects in some way the visual environment in which the child lives and learns. Linear perspective and curve perspective are everywhere visible in the everyday world about us, and in it the geometrical shapes seem to be simplest to recognize. The materials presented to the children decreased from the size of 72-point type or larger at the beginning of the eight weeks during which the specific teaching was undertaken, to the equivalent of 12 point type for those children able to use it, the decrease in size being introduced gradually. A visual discrimination test (subsequently revised and published) was used as the tool to measure improvements in the performance of each child working on the scheme and checklists monitoring every lesson were compiled. Finally results showed that every child in the group had increased in efficiency in visual discrimination and recognition considerably beyond the expectations of the researcher, and to a degree of statistical significance well beyond that of a control group of children in another school for the blind who did not work the programme. These results appeared to fulfil the aim of improving the children's capacity to interpret what they saw; this capacity seemed to have been enhanced by giving them materials embodying discrimination cues which could be associated with previously experienced stimuli. The evidence of Hildreth (1947) suggests an ongoing development of the visual process through maturation even in the presence of anomalies which may hamper seeing; Barraga's initial study, although involving small numbers of children, does much to justify this belief that training and experience seem to act as ameliorating forces towards improving visual efficiency even in children with impairment of vision.

Both the diagnostic value of Barraga's Visual Efficiency Scale (1970) and the usefulness of the materials used in the programme as a way of developing visual skills in children with low vision have been confirmed by Tobin (1972a) although he stresses the enduring need to develop a curriculum or syllabus which can both embody the principles of a visual enhancement programme and also be appropriate to the needs of the pupils in school; it is stressed that the initial study had a teaching approach and that the lessons were planned to evoke a maximum proficiency in attention to the communication and interpretation of visual impressions. Teachers of children with limited vision will naturally question whether specific teaching along these lines is an effective way of using time at school. Already they are dealing with children who are likely to take longer in performing a number of perceptual tasks than those who have no sight impairment; already they may be coping with groups of mixed visual competence, some appearing to benefit from low vision aids, and some with visual conditions for which such aids are not suitable; the presence of different levels of ability, the evidence in some cases of a developmental lag, and in others of additional handicaps and impairments in a class of visually handicapped children, necessitate much individual attention for each child in a group that seems far from homogeneous. Is there justification, therefore, in introducing an additional element of teaching and assessment into an already complex teaching situation?

It must be emphasized in addition to these considerations, that training in visual enhancement is not a specifically pre-reading or pre-writing programme. It may be the case that a child who has been considered as a braille user will be able to use print for reading after he has learned to use his vision more effectively, but leading a child on to print reading from braille reading is a possible sequel and not an essential aim of this training. The

51

rationale is to help the child with a visual handicap improve a capacity that underlies many skills before they harden into curriculum areas. With the low vision child this facility cannot be left to chance, nor can it be ensured that he will acquire it incidentally, but the claim is that the more a child looks, particularly at objects or materials at close range, the more he stimulates the pathways to the brain; as the basis of an educational philosophy underlying the teaching of visually handicapped children this is the complete swing of the pendulum away from the positive discouragement in using residual vision that was once imposed on some children; and yet it is a step further forward than simply providing a wealth of visually attractive material in the classroom to which the child might, or might not, give attention. Rather it is a form of guided discovery in which the pupil is actively involved in using his vision.

'Look and Think' project developed in Great Britain   Enthusiasm for this dynamic approach in helping children to use and enhance their visual capacities rather than to neglect or ignore them has burgeoned in several educational programmes internationally. In Great Britain teachers of the College of Teachers of the Blind conducted a survey (1973) throughout residential schools for the blind including Sunshine Homes for Nursery School Children, and Centres of Further Education and Training. This showed that of the 1,256 children and young persons registered blind in these establishments, only 583 had less than perception of light. Since it is considered that even children with very low acuity may derive some benefit from specific training in visual enhancement an exciting challenge was evident. In 1974 a Schools Council Project was initiated with the purpose of constructing a teaching programme for children with low vision and partial sight which would embody training techniques in prescribed areas of visual activity. It is envisaged that a scale to measure the level of visual efficiency will also act as a barometer of possible improvement. The involvement of teachers in schools for the blind and the partially sighted and those on the specialized course for teachers of the visually handicapped at the University of Birmingham, has bonded the theoretical with the practical in a teaching scheme whose aim is a hopeful one for children with low vision.

This scheme entitled the 'Look and Think' programme in Great

Britain may be described as a curriculum development project on the training of residual vision in the case of educationally blind and partially sighted children. The rationale underlying this is to encourage children within these categories to use any residual vision that they may possess as effectively as possible, as against the now historic approach of seeking to protect any remaining vision by limiting procedures and materials to those demanding a minimum level of visual activity. The training set out in the programme is systematic and through seeking to strengthen the development of visual skills should result in an increase both in the amount and in the quality of experience that the child enjoys. The negative effect on skilled performance in areas of visual perception resulting from lack of stimulation was measured by Hebb (1937) whilst Gibson (1953) was able to demonstrate an improvement in acuity, discrimination and also in the recognition of patterns. Barraga (1964) directed the implications of these conclusions towards the training of visually handicapped children, especially those who may be described as possessing 'low vision'.

In 1974 the Schools Council launched a three-year project under the direction of Chapman and Tobin in order to develop and evaluate materials for training children in the effective use of residual vision. The project also aimed at training teachers in the theoretical and practical application of these techniques through films and video-tapes, short courses, and teachers' workshops. The work culminated in the production of a teacher's handbook incorporating lesson plans and suggestions for alternative materials and activities, as well as giving guide-lines on recording and evaluating the pupil's progress and clarifying the objectives of the work.

The scheme takes the child through the process of recognizing and naming three-dimensional objects, with follow-up questions on such aspects as the size, shape, and function of the article examined. This is followed by work on the recognition of models of a variety of objects such as a motorbike, a bath, and a horse, since visually handicapped children sometimes have difficulty in this sort of recognition. Six sections based on discrimination follow these intitial exercises. The differences in the objects presented may be slight, requiring a simple scan-and-search strategy, but an understanding of relational concepts is also required. The programme now leads on to matching objects to sample, involving the ability to use concepts of 'alike' and 'different' as well as calling on the visual capacity to note differences in the size and shape in the objects presented.

After this, two-dimensional representation is introduced with matching of pictures. This is a particularly interesting item, since some visually handicapped children have had little experience with books and pictures and may show hesitation and uncertainty in attempting to match them. The idea of perspective is introduced next with the use of cards depicting simple pictures illustrating this phenomenon. The next exercise consists of four cards in which only the critical features of the objects have been drawn. The child is asked to attempt to identify each object. In order to help the subject make effective use of illustrative material, photographs are then introduced showing familiar objects for recognition, then drawings with questions to elicit the child's comprehension of what is depicted in them. Cards illustrating the perception of symmetry are followed by those requiring a perception of pattern. These are followed by photographs which help in the classification of facial expressions, showing anger, happiness and sadness and by body postures. The perception of gestures and body movement must result from demonstrations by the teacher, head-shaking, yawning, and walking on tip-toe are some of the actions shown. Items concerned with hand-eye co-ordination involve a pencil and paper maze and small magnets on a magnetic board. Colour differentiation and colour-naming items are then introduced with the use of seven tablets for matching and naming colours.

The teacher's handbook gives detailed instructions, stressing that the checklist based upon the activities described should be administered to one child at a time, without a time limit, but with attention to appropriate lighting, and with the child choosing the working position most comfortable for him. It is not necessary for the whole of the inventory to be completed in one session; the ophthalmologist's report on the child and the teacher's own experience and judgment should be deciding factors with regard to the length of sessions on this work.

Much of the work in developing and co-ordinating the use of materials and in evaluating them in schools for the blind and the partially sighted throughout Great Britain was undertaken by

Tooze, the Research Fellow working with the project. He had the ready co-operation of heads and staff of schools and the encouragement of the College of Teachers of the Blind and the National Association for the Education of the Partially Sighted. Hopefully, this co-operation will result in a more stimulating future for many children with low vision.

4   The school years for visually handicapped children

Some implications of visual handicap in school learning

A positive philosophy for the visually handicapped pupil and one to encourage his efforts will be that most of the educational goals set for the fully sighted will not be unattainable for him on account of his lack of vision or because of its impairment. But the pupil who has little or no sight is likely to have heavy demands made upon him in reaching comparable measurable standards of school success, although this may culminate in the passing of externally set and evaluated examinations, in some cases up to university entrance level. Examination successes at all levels are likely to rank high as criteria of effective education in the view of many parents, since they are quotable and comparable tokens of achievement shared with their child's fully sighted friends, brothers and sisters; they may also open up opportunities for further education or widen career choices.

But, of course, measurable academic successes are not sole, or in some cases even prime, educational goals, and realistic appraisal of the means by which the visually handicapped pupil can be provided with the means of achieving his optimum potential require careful consideration. The question of stress in the case of the blind and also the partially sighted pupil is discussed by Williams (1973) and also by Kell (1973). A diminished or non-existent visual input combined in some instances, as in braille reading, with a slower working rate may indicate that either an extended period of education or small group and sometimes individual tutelage are desirable if pupils with severe visual handicaps are eventually to attain the educational levels of which they are capable. Difficulties in the presentation of materials can be minimized if these are thought out in terms of the pupil's visual competence as well as in respect of his other assets or deficits. The question of relevance of content in the curriculum is a complex one since some contexts may have a different frame of reference for visually handicapped pupils than for the fully sighted in cases where they may or may not have a reservoir of visual memories upon which to draw.

Whether he is in a special school, a unit, or in an ordinary class, the visually handicapped child will be within a group of pupils with a range of visual competence including varying limitations of visual experience. His teacher must be aware of this in planning and presenting work and will need to contrive circumstances accordingly.

Presentation of learning material   Pupils who see poorly or who do not see at all are in particular need of definition of purpose and clarity of instruction from their teachers. Impaired vision or total lack of vision carry the possibility of increasing the difficulty for the pupil of knowing what is expected of him. Gesture and other forms of non-verbal communication can be indistinct or lost to such pupils, whereas the fully sighted have the opportunity of noting almost incidentally many visual signals which reinforce or amplify verbal explanations or descriptions. In addition, the pupil with a visual handicap may not be able to see or may only see imperfectly the way in which other children are tackling the learning tasks expected from them. Child-centred discovery activities are likely to require more guidance for the visually handicapped than for the fully sighted child. It cannot safely be assumed that verbal references to objects or actions familiar to the fully sighted will be clear to the blind or visually defective, although their manipulation of language may mask deficiencies of experience. Clouds and distant mountains familiar in actuality, or at least in illustration or television representation to the seeing child, can be bafflingly difficult to describe in meaningful terms to those who have never seen them clearly – or perhaps at all. Even detail taken for granted by the fully sighted such as the composition of a wall from separate bricks held together with cement, was not understood by a visually impaired 14 year old who had a good level of general intelligence and application likely to bring him examination successes. Thus it is evident that the teacher will need to develop considerable skill in helping the visually handicapped child to relate references to known and experienced contexts as well as to help him to increase his understanding of the

57

environment. Solely verbal descriptions may not be enough to clarify a reference but care must be exercised in presenting diagrammatic material, whether in embossed form for tactile discrimination or in clearly presented visual form. Over-laboured presentations can sometimes confuse rather than clarify an issue.

In presenting diagrammatic material, its relevance in conveying information to the visually handicapped is of prime importance. This very obvious teaching point can, surprisingly, be underestimated, especially in two-dimensional work, since the eye loves detail which confuses the finger.

Since the visually handicapped pupil's means of recording or receiving information can be time-consuming it is vital that he has sufficient time to complete his tasks so that he does not build up a frustrating accumulation of unfinished assignments. The pupil who is unfortunate enough to suffer from a deteriorating visual condition is in particular need of the adaptation of circumstances and presentation of material, perhaps on a temporary basis, so that he is still in a situation of being able to complete tasks successfully; the use of the tape-recorder is particularly valuable at such a juncture. The adventitiously blind pupil also will need to be presented with learning situations in which he can succeed, and in this case too, auditorily presented material is particularly valuable during the period when the fluent reading of braille has not yet been achieved.

Special techniques Both the teacher in the special school, and the peripatetic teacher or adviser giving support in a unit or mainstream school require a secure mastery of the techniques and adaptations needed in presenting materials and information for visually handicapped pupils, and also a knowledge of how these can be effectively employed in helping the pupil's learning. The presentation of adapted materials in itself represents only part of the solution to some of the learning problems. Skill and guidance in their use will also often be needed to obtain the greatest use in furthering the pupil's understanding and competence in handling and comprehending adapted material. The ability of the teacher to do this will call upon a blend of training, insight, and experience in meeting the needs of visually handicapped children.

There is a good deal of commercially available material that is well suited to the needs of visually handicapped pupils such as

Colour Factor mathematical apparatus, but for a child who sees little or nothing this may be used in a manner slightly different from the way in which it is handled by fully sighted children. There is some expertly designed specialized apparatus available such as the miniature light probe which emits a sound varying in levels according to the density of the object at which it is beamed. Simpler adaptations such as the special geometry set or the adapted Japanese abacus (Cranmer) are listed in the catalogue of apparatus and games obtainable from the Royal National Institute for the Blind. Highly sophisticated adapted apparatus even includes a 'talking calculator'. In curriculum areas with some practical bias, such as the sciences, home economics, and craftwork, apparatus and equipment can also be drawn from both commercial and specialized sources provided that it is carefully considered in terms of its use by those who are visually impaired. The general movement in education which emphasizes the child's learning through activity has resulted in the production of much colourful, three-dimensional material such as scales, varied shapes and containers which are well suited for the child with little vision, provided that he has the materials presented at a stage appropriate for his learning.

Tactile material For the pupil who is a braille user, a first essential is that the braille material with which he is presented, whether teacher-made or produced by volunteer transcribers, should be totally accurate and set out with a layout designed for finger reading and not for visual appeal. In the case of braille, an extra dot slipped in by mistake, a dot missing, or a contraction wrongly used, can alter the entire meaning of a word or phrase to a much greater extent than a spelling mistake in print. A knowledge of the different types of equipment and methods of embossing braille is useful to the teacher since although the upward braille writer is standard equipment in the UK, the small hand-frame and stylus still has some value as a quiet, unobtrusive and portable means of taking notes that can supplement the use of the portable tape-recorder.

The Thermo form machine which, by a thermo-vacuum process, enables embossed copies of raised maps and diagrams to be produced on plastic sheets speedily and in any quantity, has greatly facilitated the provision of appropriate diagrammatic work

THE SCHOOL YEARS FOR VISUALLY HANDICAPPED CHILDREN

for children using their touch modality to interpret information. Devising and reproducing material can be so fascinating that it can tempt the teacher into being almost over-ingenious so that the resultant work is overcrowded with a diversity of texture and detail.

Adaptations for pupils with some vision The visually handicapped pupil in an ordinary class can benefit from having 'desk copies' of tactile or clearly printed diagrammatic material available at the same time as blackboard or visual aids are being used in the classroom. Co-operation between the regular teacher and specialists in visual handicap is needed here so that the visually handicapped pupil is not unnecessarily in a 'remedial' situation by going over work previously undertaken by his classmates, but rather he should be using his adapted materials simultaneously with the sighted children in the group.

Whilst the value of low-vision aids has gained significance for some pupils with poor sight, and may be a factor in determining whether a pupil needs to learn braille or not, other means of helping to clarify visually presented material to pupils who have some vision should not be neglected and these may often involve a combination of appropriate illumination, working position, and the use of closed circuit television and tape-recorded material. Attention to techniques in visual search and scanning may also be needed for some pupils.

Classroom organization Some aspects of classroom organization can help to lessen the likelihood of stressful situations or confusion for pupils with problems in seeing. For these children it is helpful that there should be clear indications in advance when a lesson or an activity is about to come to an end, so that each pupil can gather up his own belongings and return them to their appropriate places. The development of orderly habits with regard to the storage and retrieval of equipment and working materials helps in the subsequent location and retrieval of these for future use, minimizing confused searching and waste of time. So far as possible the visually handicapped pupil should be increasingly responsible for fetching and retrieving his own books and work; desks, shelves, and cupboards labelled in braille and clear print and the opportunity to explore and locate landmarks in a classroom will facilitate this. If furniture or storage places are altered, he should be forewarned of this. Undue passivity and dependence on others may result if either a teacher or better sighted pupils invariably undertake the collection and distribution of materials whilst the less well seeing child simply receives it. It can be difficult for the blind or poorly seeing child to know when and how to ask for help when it is needed and to reject it without offence when it is not. The classroom situation can provide a good basis for such crucial social training.

Teaching points   In the midst of all the technical advances it may be all too easy to neglect the teacher's own contribution. The teacher's voice, use of vocabulary, and manipulation of language would seem particularly valuable in motivating the child who sees little or nothing. Clear enunciation, as well as an audible and interesting voice are considerable assets since boredom can be a hazard to the child for whom visual stimuli are reduced or absent. It can be salutary for the teacher to tape-record and then listen to a lesson and note any cliché-ridden approaches, inaudible or inexplicit directions or over-long descriptions which occur.

The pupil who is visually handicapped will need to learn some skills systematically that the fully sighted can usually pick up incidentally such as orientation, mobility, and travel skills. Some of the methods he must use for his day-to-day classwork will be very time-consuming; some concepts taken for granted by the fully sighted may present difficulties for him. He may be in a class where the teacher is anxious to help him but because of unfamiliarity with the problems of visual handicap or lack of specialized training or even information does not know how to set about this in a constructive way.

In the ensuing passages attention is drawn to some of the specific areas in which the visually handicapped pupil is likely to need specialized adaptations and an understanding of his needs. In whatever educational setting he is working, it is important that these special needs should be both well understood and realistically met.

Discovery through touch

The most evident, and perhaps to some people the most interesting aspect of learning by touch, is the tactile reading of braille but this highly specialized and refined use of the sense is only one of the ways in which information can be transmitted by the fingertips. Nor are the fingertips the only transmitters of messages about the characteristics of materials and objects to be explored. The connection between movement and the interpretation of information through touch must be appreciated so that learning situations can be presented in which the child has ample opportunity to move his fingers over learning material that has been organized in terms of touch discrimination. The ability to discriminate fine tactile detail in two-dimensional form and to interpret embossed symbols represents a culmination of skills which need to be preceded by activities of a more generalized nature. These will embody larger movements in the exploration of a variety of three-dimension objects whose form and texture can be examined in kinaesthetic terms. The environment holds a wealth of different surfaces – the rough bark of trees, the grainy texture of wood, the cold smoothness of plastic, and the warm tackiness of new bread. But usually it is through sight that the attention is drawn to these interesting things; comparisons of the qualities that objects present to the touch, their roughness, coolness, weight, or viscosity will not take place automatically in the case of the child who does not see. The pupil's curiosity may need to be aroused by verbal intervention, sound cues that attract attention and action learning involving the handling and manipulation of materials. Discussion can ensue with regard to the attributes of the object or surfaces being explored, the size, shape, texture, weight, and flexibility compared with that encountered in previous tactile discoveries. The identification of critical features, including texture patterns, direction of raised lines and shapes, and easily discriminated symbols can follow. In due course classification should follow as a result of a consideration of the function or representation embodied in the object which can be compared with previous experiences in tactile recognition. Only after sufficient opportunity has been given for activities in relating tactile exploration of varied three-dimensional forms can the presentation of two-dimensional surface representation be meaningful.

Tactile activities in play   Early activities in the pre-school and early school years can provide excellent opportunities for tactile discovery through play. The hands need to be used in different ways, in strong movements of pulling and pushing which help to give strength and flexibility as well as in the later finer movements involved in surface discrimination by the fingertips.

It is not unusual to find that congenitally blind children in particular have considerable difficulty in handling and manipulating materials that seem easy to deal with by the fully sighted. Cutting out cardboard or stiff paper with scissors, for instance, can provide difficulty, so can holding and using cutlery at mealtimes. The fingers may not have been used in different ways in manipulation and so seem weak and flabby. Clay or plasticine pushed about with the hands into balls or sausages, the use of finger puppets, the use of commercially available manipulative toys, building blocks and nesting cubes can all be helpful. More structured activities include shape matching with wooden or plastic geometric forms, and texture matching with pieces of fabric with interesting surfaces to feel which can be glued to cards. However, as with attempts in other areas to stimulate attention to learning through using the senses, a rigid over-programmed approach is undesirable. The activities should help to carry forward the process of thinking and should have an enriching and interesting content that motivates towards increasing the enjoyment of tactile discovery. Handicrafts and the construction of simple models by the pupils themselves can encourage the handling and utilization of materials of varied textures and consistencies in a creative way.

Drawings and diagrams in tactile form   More specifically, and at a later stage in schooling, Pickles (1966) advocates both the value and viability of drawing for the blind, even for totally and congenitally blind pupils. He claims that after such a child has learnt to recognize objects by exploring their shapes and dimensions through touch he should be given the means of making his own diagrams. Since this process is time consuming and offers difficulties in execution, its value can be questioned but Pickles believes that it is an activity helpful both to those relying on touch alone, as well as for those using touch and vision in their understanding of embossed diagrams. The ability to use touch in this way is a skill which cuts across the curricula areas of the secondary school, for example underlying work in maths, science, and geography. The child with too little vision for making use of illustrations and visually presented diagrams is especially in need of training in understanding diagrammatic work in embossed relationships and connections, such as in the layout of a piece of laboratory apparatus. Furthermore in justifying his emphasis on undertaking surface representation for diagrammatic work, Pickles claims that executing diagrams can be one way of learning to understand their implications. With a rubber mat providing a resilient base, a sheet of aluminium foil can be used to take a negative (downward indented) line made by a ball-point pen. The Sewell apparatus (RNIB) embodies a thin film of transparent plastic sheeting stretched over a rubber-surfaced board, and again, a special ball-point pen, an ordinary biro, or a spur wheel which cuts small dot-like indentations can be used for lines. Manilla paper as used for braille writing can take imprints from a spur wheel also, and the specialized geometry set available from the RNIB enables the user to make raised geometric figures on paper. Vincent (1970) has constructed a special drawing board which enables the student to prepare perspective drawing, but it is important that the pupil's understanding of what he is attempting to do is not superseded by devices that help him to produce work only understandable in sighted terms.

Surface representation The teacher considering the question of producing surface representational diagrams is likely to turn again, to Pickles' work in *Teaching Maths and Science to the Blind* (1970). Here there are detailed step-by-step suggestions as to how to build up a master copy using string or wire for outlines and textured materials such as scrim or fine wire mesh to provide distinguishable surfaces on a firm base. The master copy thus constructed can be used in the Thermoform machine which by thermo-vacuum suction can produce copies of the diagram imprinted on thin sheets of opaque plastic. The resulting copies take the imprint of the matrix copy clearly, but there can be some lessening of the differences in texture constructed in the original diagram. In investigating the effectiveness of work produced in this way, blind pupils at Worcester College for the Blind found a rough line more distinguishable than a smooth one, a line with a triangular crest gave optimum discriminability and a diagram of about 14 cm square gave the most comfortable size for exploration by the fingers when the base of the hand was placed at the bottom of it. Moreover, a large diagram 1 m square in which arms, hands, and fingers had to be stretched out to encompass the entire width, gave some general impression of relationships, for example in the relative position of countries or continents to each other.

Enthusiasm to make the map or diagram as informative as possible can lead to overcrowding of symbols, whilst the addition of braille words in the body of the diagram causes confusion. A tactile diagram needs to have enough information to encourage exploration and interest but not so many raised lines, braille labels, and varied textures that clarity is lost. A series of maps or diagrams each displaying a particular aspect of what is to be presented provides a more comprehensible illustration. For example, several basic raised outline maps of a country can be made with additions on one version to indicate climate, on another indications of vegetation, on another population or geological features. To crowd all this information on to one map by using different raised symbols is likely to be confusing.

The information received from such presentations needs to be discussed so that misapprehensions can be cleared up, and the pupils will also need training in interpreting the symbols used. The teacher will need to draw attention verbally to the information represented and even to ensure that the map or diagram is being used the right way up. Cutting along the top of it with pinking shears gives a quick way of checking.

Histograms and graphs Whittaker (1967) gives interesting examples of ways in which tactile representation can be used in histograms. Basic work here involves the use of small toy cars and tiny dolls which can be used first on a one-to-one basis to represent a number of children in a group or, for example, the number of cars owned by parents in a class.

Increasing complexity is introduced as one object is used to represent several, one car for every ten, and then tactile symbols can replace miniature objects in indicating comparisons. Tactile representations of this kind follow on the use of Dienes Multibase or Colour Factor mathematical materials which should have helped the pupils to understand the relationships of numbers.

Three-dimensional models The value of both two-dimensional diagrammatic work and of three-dimensional models in the teaching of visually handicapped pupils is likely to be the cause of continuing discussion and examination since its effectiveness is hard to gauge. Beautifully constructed scale models of buildings or of animals may have a primarily visual appeal. Characteristic qualities of texture, temperature, or even the smell of the original, are not present in a model, but many things are impossible to bring into a classroom. Whilst first-hand experiences offer a vital form of exploration even these are not always possible. The sighted child is likely to have seen seas, mountains, and wild animals at least on television or in illustrations. So far as possible the blind child needs real experiences too, but as a supplement to these and to clarify the relationships of parts to a whole, to understand function and construction both three-dimensional and two-dimensional tactile presentation is a useful if imperfect supplement to other ways of presenting information.

Tactile exploration for the child with some vision For the child with some vision learning through touch should not be neglected. This is not simply because he may have a deteriorating visual condition which could at some time result in having to learn braille, or eventually resulting in a work situation where lighting is not ideal for using vision and thus the use of touch rather than sight is needed. Early attention through interpreting through touch may indeed help to ease difficulties in such situations should they occur later, but in any case through this sense of touch the visually handicapped child has a means of gaining fuller information and of finding out characteristics and qualities in objects so that he gains a more complete appreciation of his environment. If he uses his hearing and his haptic sense sensitively it does not follow that he will use his defective visual senses less. His teachers and parents need not fear that using his unimpaired senses will make him behave like a totally blind person. Increased awareness of touch may in fact help him to receive fuller information and a greater realization of the qualities of the objects in the world about him.

Learning to listen

Why develop listening skills?   There is no conclusive evidence to show

66

that a child who lacks visual intactness will automatically compensate for this deficit by listening with such skill and concentration that he is able to interpret environmental sounds with accuracy, and gain information which will help him in his cognitive development simply through being presented with material in auditory form. And yet investigations show that at school, if he is using braille he is likely to read at a much slower rate than a sighted child using print (Williams, 1971) and if he is partially sighted he may need to rely on auditory material as an important supplement to his print reading. The need to use broadcast and taped material effectively will be particularly important to the pupil with deteriorating vision or sudden sight loss since learning braille will take some time, while gaining information from print may be increasingly difficult or impossible for him.

Teachers of visually handicapped children tend to have anecdotal evidence of their pupil's ability to recognize people by the sound of their footsteps and to gauge their moods with accuracy from tones of voice as well as by the words used in situations of personal interaction. It would be interesting to have more hard evidence with regard to the characteristics of children with this capacity for interpreting sound and to see if it relates to pre-school activities in which parents have related sounds to objects and actions rather than giving too much unrelated sound stimulation, for example by leaving the young visually handicapped child in a room with the television on or with the wireless playing.

Listening responses in the pre-school child   Barraga (1974) suggests ways in which the young visually handicapped child may be helped to give attention to auditory stimuli by being motivated to respond to specific sounds in the environment. But she draws attention to the connection between responses to sound and the development of purposeful movement, for instance in the example of the child turning his head towards his mother when she speaks, or the toddler reaching out or walking towards a squeaking toy. In such cases, a perception of position and distance is being developed as a result of sound, but even more important is the relationship of auditory information to language and conceptual development. In emphasizing this connection Barraga discounts the value of training schemes which call for the repetition of meaningless sounds and words since she considers that they may simply reinforce the tendency for severely visually handicapped children to imitate words and phrases without any attention to their content.

Auditory activities in school   However, in the case of children who have not had help before they come to school in learning to relate sounds to actions, events, and people in an increasingly meaningful way, a structured programme may be helpful in motivating them to give attention to sound cues through a series of games and activities. The programme outlined by Bishop (1971) suggests such an approach to help the young visually handicapped child to enhance his ability to succeed in simple sound identification and thence to develop a greater ability in his powers of listening with discrimination. Beginning with simple examples such as the sound of a spoon in a cup or of a book being closed, the suggested schemes continue with taped recordings of a telephone ringing or a clock ticking followed by identification of the voices of different speakers; exercises in tonal and volume discrimination include recognition of the differences between near and far, high and low, loud and soft sounds. Traditional stories can provide excellent material for recognizing the different sound in voices of individual characters as in *The Three Bears* and *The Three Trees*. Sound and rhythm replication can be practised in 'Do As I Do' games. Discrimination between words that sound similar but not identical can be the means of leading into a phonic programme, but the aim should be to progress as quickly as possible into work that involves the comprehension of auditory material rather than simply presenting sound for identification, location and discrimination of tone and volume.

Tape-recorded material   Good quality taped material is easily available but the teacher needs to consider this carefully and to clarify the purpose for which it is being used. It is essential to listen to the tape beforehand to ensure that the content is not beyond the experiential level of the visually handicapped pupils using it. Appropriate introductory work and questions and activities designed to follow up the taped material will reinforce the content. Pupils may find it difficult to deal with the taped material if it contains a density of facts or complex references, but narrative and dramatic material and poetry are well suited to this means of presentation.

Some attempts have been made to analyse the different levels of attention involved in listening, particularly to taped material, by blind people. In the Upsala Pedagogiska Project, Trowald (1975) investigated listening strategies for blind secondary school pupils, concluding that there are three activity levels in listening, and suggesting that an understanding of these can be of value in helping visually handicapped pupils to increase their capacity to gain information from material presented in auditory form. He describes hearing as a relatively low-level activity, in some ways equivalent to seeing whilst he considers listening to involve a greater degree of mental activity comparable to observing; he uses the term 'auding' to describe a higher level of mental processing of recorded sound which includes listening with analytical ability and critical reasoning and thus there is some resemblance to the thinking processes involved in attentive reading.

In view of the necessity for the visually handicapped pupil to use auditory material as a means of learning, the techniques which Trowald puts forward for increasing efficiency in this work warrant careful attention by the teacher of such pupils. As reference work and textbook information play an increasing part in the secondary school and further education curriculum, the visually handicapped pupil will need to use taped material more and more as a central means of input if he is blind and using braille texts which may sometimes be difficult to obtain or can be slow to read; they will offer a supplementary means of obtaining information if he is partially sighted.

Techniques for improving listening efficiency Trowald (1975) recommends that rather than having periods of unbroken listening to recorded material the pupil should, instead, stop the tape at intervals and construct questions about the content of the material he is using. One tape recorder can be used for playing the recorded material whilst another is used for taping questions. Suggested answers can be recorded on a second track on the tape on the latter machine. A complex process such as this presupposes that the pupil has been taught how to handle the machine skilfully. The use of a tape recorder with a variable speed control gives the listener the opportunity to increase the speed, and in some ways this replicates the process of skimming in reading. In fact, this researcher observed that the blind pupils in his study preferred to listen to taped material at 50 per cent higher speed than normal speaking; while the speed preferred by fully sighted children was 20 per cent faster than normal speaking; in both cases the preferred speed varied with the difficulty of the text. The blind pupils showed less fatigue and maintained their level of comprehension, whilst the comprehension of the sighted children diminished towards the end of the tape.

Visually handicapped pupils will need to develop efficient study techniques through listening in order to gain specific information and to acquire the ability to practise selective listening. Concentration against a background of distracting sound and eventually the highly developed skill of evaluative listening can be achieved. Sound advertisements and propaganda broadcasts provide material for discussion and for developing discrimination between claims, opinions, and facts.

The language laboratory provides a learning situation and a group activity useful for more than learning foreign languages. It can be successfully used for auditory taped work of the kind described above and for the pupils to read and play back their own creative oral expression. Tape recorders with one or more plug-in earpieces can be used in part of a classroom for project work; this has been a successful method used in mathematics for working out problems orally, and because of the facility for recording it gives more opportunity for self-criticism in oral work than ephemeral discussion. The portable tape-recorder can be used as a 'sound diagram' giving directions for following a specified route in mobility.

The student in further education will be particularly dependent on listening and using taped material in his work but he will have been greatly helped if, during his school days, he has received training and practice in making maximum use of his powers of attentive and discriminating listening.

Reading and writing in braille

Development of tactile codes for reading Early attempts to present

70

letters or words in a tactile way so that they could be interpreted by the blind present a wealth of ingenious forms evidencing varying degrees of effectiveness. These ranged from different shaped knots in string, to modified capital letters embossed and large enough to be discriminated by the fingers. The two embossed codes which have stood the test of time are known as Moon and Braille. The former which bears some approximation to a raised form of large-print letters is not used in schools, but since 1872 braille has been the established code in educational as well as in most other areas where symbolic communication is used by and for the blind. This code was adapted by Louis Braille from an eight-dot form to a six-dot form; the original was a means of secret communication used in the French army and described by its inventor, Charles Barbier, as *écriture nocturnal*.

Its disadvantages in the modern educational setting are that it is bulky and in its contracted form it has arbitrary rules not in line with current vocabulary usage. But it has advantages also which have stood the test of time in over a century of international usage.

Indeed, the eventual mastery of braille reading is a complex skill which includes the memorizing of a code based on the permutation of six raised dots which form the braille cell. Despite disadvantages this six-dot form of communication is remarkable since both a mathematics and music code have been developed from it as well as the two basic forms generally used for reading. The first of these, 'Grade I' or uncontracted braille, consists of a braille symbol for each letter of the alphabet. The form of braille normally used for reading, however, is referred to as 'Grade II' and when used in this way the dots are employed in different combinations which can be used for syllables of words or indeed in some cases for whole words. These representations are referred to as 'braille contractions' and their usage is governed by a series of quite complex, and indeed at times, apparently arbitrary rules.

Pre-reading activities What constitutes 'reading readiness' for the child who will need to use braille as his medium of literacy? As for the sighted child, a vital consideration will be his level of language development and the need not only to be able to read and write but to have something to read and write about. But there are a number of additional factors to consider in the case of the child using braille. He will need his own kind of pre-reading

71

programme giving attention to communication through language and first-hand experience in exploring objects. Whereas most sighted children will have newspapers, magazines, books, posters and slogans at least within their visual environment if still beyond their full comprehension, this will not be the case for the child who is blind. The blind child's association of words with actions, objects and events, may need particular attention before he is ready to link the symbols of braille characters with spoken words. The pupil who is to become a proficient braille reader needs to develop skill in the tactile discrimination of small forms as well as to have developed a sufficient use of language to appreciate meaningful content presented in the code. Powers of both short- and long-term memory will be needed in order to retain the impression of the configuration of the symbols and to remember when and in what circumstances the contracted form of the code may be used. Thus it will be readily understood that a heavy cognitive load, together with the need for fine tactile discrimination, is imposed on children who must use this form of symbolic communication as their means of literacy. In addition as Lorimer (1975) has indicated, the pad of the pupil's finger usually deals with only one braille cell at a time and the ability to perceive the symbols for the word as a whole thus increasing speed and encouraging contextural guessing is not possible for a finger-reader in the same way as for the sighted reader who has many more cues available simultaneously.

Lowenfeld's comprehensive study, published in book form (1969) as *Blind Children Learn to Read*, enumerates the type of pre-reading skills that he has found helpful in developing the necessary requisites for reading braille by the young child. These include matching and sorting objects of different shapes and discriminating textures. The left-to-right movement of the hands can be encouraged with games and puzzles involving following a raised line with the fingers.

Teaching of braille reading to schoolchildren   In view of such problems for the pupil learning braille it is not surprising that a number of studies have been undertaken in which the characteristics of effective and accurate braille readers have been observed, and the problems of those finding the task difficult or impossible have been investigated.

In the UK a survey on braille attainment undertaken by Williams (1971) and incorporated as a substantial item in the report of the Vernon Committee (1972) focused attention on the most evident causes of lack of success in the teaching of braille reading. It was emphasized strongly in this study that the outstanding difficulty for pupils in school was their reading rate. The level of comprehension did not differ significantly from that of sighted children of comparable age on the Ballard Silent Reading Test, but 40 per cent of the blind children in a sample of 488 subjects between the ages of 10 and 16 were unsuccessful in completing the reading test, and the average rate for silent reading was between 80 to 100 words per minute, about half that for sighted pupils. Williams gave detailed consideration to the sources of failure amongst the children tested, and concluded that both absence from school at critical learning periods and late admission to a school for the blind had been contributory causes in a substantial number of cases. Factors relating to the way in which braille was regarded also had a bearing on failure, especially in cases of low motivation on the part of the pupil, lack of sufficient practice in reading, the absence of a consistent policy of teaching braille throughout the school, and an insufficiently positive attitude towards braille reading on the part of the teacher. Low mental ability was an important contributory factor in the difficulties of some 25 per cent of the pupils considered whilst a few had the additional problem of slight spasticity in the hand. Indeed a careful observation of the hand movements of the readers in this study was one of the most fascinating aspects of it, since the researcher carefully noted whether her subjects used one or both hands in reading, which fingers were used predominantly, whether the pressure exerted was light or heavy, and whether up or down movements of a searching nature were used. The fast readers had a number of characteristics in common which should receive attention in the teaching of braille reading. The movement of the hands was light and skimming, 72 per cent of the fast readers used both hands for reading and there was a tendency for them to have other fingers besides the predominating one on the line of symbols. The slow readers evidenced less skilful, searching movements and in a number of cases were children who had not concentrated fully on either print or braille but were somewhat divided in their attention between these two forms of presentation. Williams's findings with regard to hand movements are in accord with those of Lowenfeld (1969) and also with a more recent study in the Netherlands by Mommers (1975) who also noted that the quicker, more successful pupils reading braille did not rub the dots in scrubbing movements, were less likely to lose their places on the line, had good posture, with only slight pressure on the fingers as they passed over the dots with a flowing movement. He also confirmed the connection between a good level of intelligence and successful reading, but found no significant affect on technical reading competence as a result of the degree of blindness.

Reading speeds and comprehension in children using braille A major investigation into the competence of pupils using braille in schools in the UK, undertaken by Lorimer (1975) considered both comprehension and speed and resulted in conclusions highly relevant to the curriculum of blind pupils. Williams's 1971 study had given rise to concern with regard to the attainment of braille reading among pupils and Lorimer considered that although teachers usually had small groups of pupils and thus had a considerable knowledge of their pupils' individual progress, nevertheless it was desirable that there should be a means of objective measurement of their attainment in braille reading. Two useful tests were already in use throughout schools for the blind. The Tooze Speed Test (1962) for pupils between 7 and 13 years which gave 120 words of three letters to be scanned for speed, and the Lorimer Recognition Test (1962) offering 174 braille contractions to be used for word recognition for the same age-group. Lorimer finally chose the Neale (1958) Analysis of Reading which presents graded reading for the 6- to 12-year-old group of sighted children. This test has the advantage of parallel forms to permit re-testing, and indicates age norms for accuracy, reading rate, and comprehension. In using a braille version of this test throughout schools for the blind in Great Britain, Lorimer confirmed earlier findings that it was in the rate of reading that braille users were at a considerable disadvantage compared with those using print. Although there was some retardation in comprehension with the braille user the gap between the blind and sighted narrowed in the upper age group. The blind were also slower than the sighted in word recognition skills. Lorimer confirmed the fact that the size of the fingertip as a conductor of information limits speed in reading, so that in the case of his subjects it was observed that even better touch readers were achieving about 55 per cent of the reading speed of average sighted readers. An important aspect of this research lies in the recommendation for dealing with some of the difficulties inherent in a braille teaching scheme. For instance, the researcher recommends a consistent teaching policy throughout the school with remedial programmes for those pupils who need this, including stress on a good knowledge of the code. This could be improved, he states, by systematic character recognition training and speed training in the secondary as well as in the primary school. He also recommends specific reading courses for those requiring academic or commercial approaches to their work and regular objective appraisal of the progress of all pupils.

Grade I and Grade II braille   Since the braille code can be used in the two forms, Grade I uncontracted and Grade II contracted, there have been different approaches over the years with regard to presenting the material to beginners. The two divergent policies with regard to the introduction of braille are described by Hechle (1974).

The teachers who have favoured using Grade I at the beginning of reading schemes leaving Grade II until the uncontracted form has been mastered, might well claim that this method gives the child the opportunity of reading experience without having to cope with the complexities of contractions at an early stage and gives encouragement for the fingers to move along the line. Precedence is given in this teaching approach to the phonic element and to word-building practice in reading. On the other hand, a child who learns words in their contracted form from the start learns them in the form in which he will subsequently always encounter them without re-learning.

Specialized braille reading schemes for children   Finding appropriate material in braille, well suited in content for beginners, has posed a problem. Books that look easy in print can contain a surprising number of quite difficult contractions when transcribed into Grade II braille. Teaching approaches have been reflected in the choice of reading schemes for transcribing from print. Attempts have been made to introduce contractions gradually or to use a number of reading schemes in which graded books for the sighted were transcribed for the blind. However, teachers in schools for the blind in the UK were convinced that a specialized reading scheme was needed which would take cognizance of the particular difficulties of the braille code especially with regard to its contractions. They wanted readable material that the pupils would enjoy as well as being relevant to the vocabulary of young blind children. Tobin (1972b) undertook a study of the written and spoken vocabulary used by 132 young blind children.

Vocabulary of young blind children   It was felt that a braille reading scheme for beginners must give real attention to the vocabulary that children knew and used. The limiting effect of word lists as a basis for reading is well understood but it is stressed by Tobin that in the case of blind children who need to learn a reading code by using fingertips which take up information at a slower rate than the eye, it is especially important that difficulties be reduced to a minimum and an added burden of new topics and unfamiliar words might militate against the ease of reading experience. Tobin's study includes a searching review of previous work on the language development of blind children highlighting the noticeable verbalism sometimes encountered. He also notes that some research, including that of Hayes (1941) indicated overall 'an inferiority in the understanding of words'.

Consideration is also given to the findings of Maxfeld (1936) that blind children asked more questions, gave fewer commands and in her opinion indicated a need for security which, in some respects, could be satisfied through verbal communication. Tobin's study which took cognizance of previous studies of the vocabulary of sighted children (Burroughs, 1957) showed the extent to which the vocabularies of the sighted and the blind overlap. However, he justifiably draws attention to the fact that the repetition of frequently used words from a list results in a tedious context and suggests that the word lists compiled should rather be used as building blocks with additional pre-reading activities. An interesting analysis is given of the differences between words used by the blind and those encountered in lists of words used by the sighted children of equivalent ages. Colour words were used relatively infrequently by blind 5- and 6-year-olds but increased during the 7- to 8-year-old group who had been exposed to more diverse verbal references by teachers, classmates, and older children.

'The Family Books' In 1971 a Reading Committee set up by the College of Teachers of the Blind, composed of teachers from schools for the blind developed a specialized reading scheme in braille, bearing in mind the findings of Tobin's Vocabulary Study and also the problems arising from the contracted form of braille. After different approaches with regard to using Grade I and Grade II had been considered there was increasing agreement about the introduction of Grade II in reading from the start. The aim of the scheme was to reduce the perceptual and cognitive load of the young reader beginning to use braille. Four story sequences were composed each centred round an imaginary family. The first books used a vocabulary that did not involve words needing contractions and which were drawn from the first three of Tobin's word lists. The four schemes were parallel in their gradual and agreed introduction of words involving the use of contractions. Attention was given to the presentation of the books which were small for braille books, 22 cm × 14½ cm, and thus not too heavy or difficult for the young reader to handle. It was made clear that in order to use the readers the pupil must already be able to recognize the braille symbols as letters of the alphabet. In the first books of the series the phonic method of reading was the underlying principle. This sounding of words letter by letter with the construction of the word from the sounds is to some extent dictated by the fact that the fingertips touch the symbol one at a time in braille.

Attention was also given to sentence structure and to punctuation in the attempt to graduate the difficulties of the reading material. It is emphasized that pre-reading activities, including left to right movement of the hands, are essential as the specialized reading scheme does not attempt to introduce braille signs according to ease of recognition by touch. The gradual introduction of contractions for whole words such as 'and' or 'the' involves a 'look and say' element in reading. The later books in the series represent an attempt to introduce the complexities of Grade II braille in relation to the child's perceptual and cognitive development. The order of these consists of the introduction of pronouns, conjunctions, word signs, abbreviations, followed by an increasing number of more difficult contractions. Those familiar with the braille code and the rules for contractions and the word signs in the Grade II form will appreciate the difficulty of balancing the demands of the vocabulary level of the child, with the level of difficulty of the Grade II braille rules whilst maintaining an interesting level of material in the text. The authors of this scheme would not claim to have solved all the problems but they have developed a lively and by now widely used early reading scheme which gives realistic attention to the particular problems of braille reading for a young beginner.

Supplementary material for use with the reading scheme   The sighted child usually has his first reading books decorated with colourful and attractive pictures and it was felt that the blind child misses a delightful and motivating element in the absence of these in his braille books. Consequently an imaginative approach was made in devising supplementary material which hopefully would serve the function of increasing motivation, giving direct preparation for the next reading stage, adding material for slower readers and extending the range of the readers' experience. Greenwood (1975) was instrumental in devising and making prototype material consisting of additional tape-recorded stories, small models of villages, and large soft dolls representing the characters in the stories. The combined effort of practitioners and researchers in the development of this scheme and its supplementary material is of more than local interest. The rationale of the scheme has been referred to in some detail since it exemplifies an approach to the teaching of braille which evidences not only a knowledge of the problems involved in its teaching but also a lively awareness of the developmental needs of children as they learn to read. The practice of using the *Standard English Braille Primer* as a basis for teaching primary school children to read braille with its seven-line system and rigorous practice exercises, is by contrast quite inappropriate.

Braille reading as the pupil progresses through school   The addition to the staff of an ordinary school of 'a braille instructor' is equally dubious, since if a child's vision is so poor that he needs to use this medium for communication in reading and writing he is likely to need help from a teacher or adviser in areas that extend well beyond a knowledge of the braille code.

The young reader who has completed a specialized reading scheme can progress to a transcribed reading scheme and to a variety of reading material since it is essential to remember that braille is not literacy but rather represents the gateway to literacy in providing the means by which the blind pupil can obtain information and derive enjoyment from books. There are some excellent readers available in braille at primary school level which can be obtained from one of the branches of the National Library for the Blind and suggestions with regard to these are outlined in *Books and Blind Children* (Chapman and Wilson, 1970). It can be useful for the pupil on an individual basis to have two braille readers in his possession. One well within the scope of his reading level to get on with in his own time, in addition he can have a slightly more difficult text for which he can enlist the teacher's help during class reading periods. A regular period in the day or week when part of a book is read aloud gives shared enjoyment and pupils should be encouraged to take braille books home at weekends and to have them available in the evenings to 'find out what happens next' and dispel any impression that reading is simply for the classroom.

The need to give specific attention to braille reading and writing even in the secondary school years, is emphasized by both Mommers (1975) and Lorimer (1975) whilst Myers (1975) noted improvements in the ability of multiply handicapped blind youths to read braille if they had continued instruction even after they had left school.

The reading problem of the late blind child is a complex one, and individual teachers have worked out their own schemes. Tobin (1971) has an excellent programme based on taped material designed for the adventitiously blind adult but useful for later blind adolescents and older senior pupils.

Technical advances in tactile reading   Modern technology has been used in the production of braille material and the computer has been utilized in this connection. Braille textbooks and readers are available from the Royal National Institute for the Blind who publish a list of available titles. The University of Warwick has initiated a scheme of braille transcription from printed material for blind clients and many schools and advisers are indebted to voluntary transcribers for help in brailling texts.

However, the Vernon Report draws attention to the difficulties in supplying an adequate number of braille books for school use promptly. This is a problem which has already received serious attention but it remains an outstanding area of concern for the teacher who needs to be sure that the books required following a particular syllabus are available at the time when they are needed.

A technical development which holds promise for tactile readers is the machine known as 'the Optacon'. This sophisticated piece of apparatus can convert ordinary printed images into a corresponding tactile image, with the advantage that it is therefore not restricted to any particular type-style or language. The apparatus consists of three main sections composed of a miniature opto-electronic camera, an electronic section, and a tactile stimulator array which consists of 144 small metal rods placed in an area of about 1 cm by 2 cm and arranged in 6 columns across and 24 along. The miniature camera is able to travel along a line of print and is connected by a light cable to the electronic section of the apparatus. When the machine is in operation it is able to convert the image of the printed letter into a pattern of vibrating rods which can be interpreted by the finger. Tobin *et al.* (1973) reporting on trials of this machine consider that initial and continuing practice with graded materials on a regular basis is necessary and that learning its usage is in the same order of difficulty as that presented to some adult readers in learning braille. Younger readers given the opportunity of a daily basic training period with additional free practice might gain benefit and pilot schemes are in operation at the grammar schools for blind pupils.

Successful use of such equipment brings a new dimension of experience to blind readers and necessitates the development of new educational techniques. However, whatever means are used for the transmission of written symbols to the reader the need for sound basic educational principles continues with the encouragement of motivation towards reading and the development of good levels of comprehension with regard to the material presented.

Learning to write braille Many teachers begin the process of braille writing with their pupils at the same time as they begin reading. Most pre-reading activities are simultaneously pre-writing activities. The time spent in exploring shape and texture and in interpreting and discriminating sounds is helping to give the child something to write about. If the young visually handicapped child has had the advantage of early opportunities in associating words with objects and actions he will have a start in his reading and writing readiness programme. A sense of pattern and an association of pattern with meaning will have to be developed. Pittam (1965) outlines an approach in which patterns which will later represent braille letter combinations can be used. In addition to tactile and, if circumstances permit it, visual enhancement, auditory readiness needs to be developed. Story telling by the teacher, re-telling of the story by the pupils, gives attention to the building up of sequence. The acting out of stories can be tied in with the actual and imagined events in the child's life, and it must of course be ensured that the visually handicapped child has enough opportunities of real conversation with adults outside the classroom as well as with his playmates. This is a particular challenge to be met in the residential situation where the ratio of adults to children in out of school hours may be much lower than in the family situation.

Indeed in considering some of the difficulties involved in the writing of braille by beginners, Hechle (1975) concludes that an understanding of language structure is a vital element which may have to be built up over a period of careful and considered tutelage. The mechanics of the process of writing braille offer fewer problems now than in the past in that with the use of an Upward Braille Writer such as the Perkins Writer, the dots are embossed on to thick manilla paper in the same form in which they are read. Previous methods involved indenting the dots with the necessity for the learner to memorize the characters in reverse for writing. Some senior pupils and students still find a use for a stylo and small hand frame for note-taking when the use of an upward writer would be inconvenient, but the use of a portable tape recorder has minimized this need.

Hechle however, exposes a central difficulty which teachers may encounter when children wish to write a sentence that is within the structure of their spoken language but which involves a complex use of contractions that lie beyond the range of their reading experience. He refers to the three ways in which this eventuality may be met as being to allow the child to write as he thinks fit without undue attention to correctness in the braille form or to show the child the correct form even if this involves difficult contractions at the limit or beyond the limit of his comprehension. Finally an attempt may be made to restrict the child's writing within the structures and attainments of his reading levels. The blind child is less likely than the sighted to encounter the written word incidentally and he is also restricted by the fact that finger reading reduces predictability. Over-restriction to ensure correct braille forms in the early stages of writing is undesirable and the use of a scheme such as *The Family Books* as a test on which to draw for practice in written answers to questions is helpful in that it embodies the controlled introduction of contractions.

Oral and written communication should develop side by side. The correction of mistakes in written braille needs to be undertaken on an individual basis and with care not to discourage the fluency of imaginative content of the pupil's expression. Blind pupils often appear to enjoy using the braille upward writer and learn to handle it with skill. Whilst encouraging accuracy and speed in the use of the braille code in all its complexity the pupil's creative expression must not be stifled. Exposure to correct forms of written braille and ample opportunity to practise writing it are vital aspects in helping the pupil to use this medium effectively to convey his thoughts in symbolic form.

Print reading and writing for pupils with defective vision

Visual skills involved in reading print   In a classroom where children with defective sight are using printed books, not braille, for reading, we might find John whose near vision is very poor so that the page of his book is held so close in reading that it touches his nose; Bill who has cataracts but is receiving treatment for this condition with a consequent improvement in the amount he can see; Jill who is an albino and who hates books with bright shiny pages, and Kim whose eye condition involving macula degeneration affects his central vision. In addition to these physically based visual problems the teacher suspects that some of her pupils have specific reading disabilities not entirely attributable to their visual defects. Also, Bill's hospital attendances have meant rather frequent absence from school, Kim comes from a socially deprived area, and Jill, although an albino, is an immigrant child with a limited vocabulary in English.

But all these pupils will need to develop comparable basic skills in order to use print for reading. They will need to be able to select a figure from its background, a letter, a group of letters or a word or phrase from the page. They will need to perceive constancy of shape in the case of letters and words presented in different sizes and type styles and to discriminate between letters that are similar in appearance. Besides developing sequential memory for visual and auditory symbols and the ability to discriminate and blend sounds, their skill in eye-hand co-ordination will need to be established and strengthened. All these skills are among those recognized as underlying the complex achievements of reading and writing and are largely associated with processes of visual perception. But the teacher concerned with reading and writing for visually handicapped pupils will want to know if there are any general principles applicable in teaching these skills to such children and if there are any specific approaches of benefit to pupils with particular visual problems.

Reading achievement in partially sighted children   One needs initially to consider whether visually handicapped children have been shown to have problems in reading greater than those of the non-handicapped child. It could be expected that visual defects limiting the visual field might well have an effect on speed and fluency. It is not surprising that research evidence shows a variety of conclusions when one considers the heterogeneous nature of visually handicapped pupils and the number of variables which, in addition to their defective sight, might influence their reading achievements. In reviewing the literature on the attainments of the partially sighted, Lansdown (1975) finds in general terms a range of evidence with regard to the learning achievement as well as to the social adjustment of these pupils. He cites several workers including Eames (1937), Park and Burri (1943), Schonell (1948), and Vernon (1971) who associate low reading ability with poor vision. There is also some evidence that partially sighted pupils may be older than fully sighted children in the same class. Peck (1925), Benton (1963), and Birch *et al.* (1966) show studies spanning the years which give confirmation of this tendency. However, complexity is introduced into the issue by the findings of such workers as Tinker (1936) and Douglas *et al.* (1968) who recorded exceptionally high reading rates among myopic children. As a sequel to his comprehensive review of previous studies a further one was undertaken by Lansdown himself (1975) with subjects from schools for the partially sighted in London matched with fully sighted pupils attending ordinary schools. His result showed no significant difference in the reading competence between the partially sighted and the fully sighted subjects but there were indications of a slower rate of achievement in other tasks involving visual perception, for instance in the copying of shapes, in which the partially sighted showed some lag. The small classes in the special schools for the partially sighted and the availability of individual help from the teacher were considered to be possible factors contributing to the relative success in reading by the partially sighted group in the study.

Visual perception in print reading   Carroll and Hibbert (1973) also draw attention to the varied nature of the problems of partially sighted pupils and the difficulty of establishing from previous research either generalized or widely accepted conclusions about the attainments of these pupils as a group. Their own study indicated that in a sample of 13 partially sighted pupils of infant and junior age the mean scores on conventional intelligence tests were slightly below the means of the comparison group. Although the sample here is small the results give some support to Fine's (1968) survey of 1,374 partially sighted pupils in special schools in the UK which showed a comparable tendency to score below the average. Carroll and Hibbert are intrigued by the possibility that perceptual ability and visual capacity could be related.

Whilst there is criticism of the approach to training visual perception from some workers, evidence such as that contributed by Carroll and Hibbert suggests that the teacher of reading to visually handicapped children needs to give attention to perceptual training as part of the teaching of reading.

A reading scheme such as *Racing to Read* devised by Tansley and Nichols (1962) offers both these elements, and is well suited to partially sighted readers in its presentation which is in a clear format, well spaced, and with simple illustrations.

Reading and Remedial Reading by Tansley (1967) again presents material useful in the early stages of reading, with its accompanying activities of matching, of left-to-right movement and emphasis of body awareness. In both these books the vocabulary and content are well suited to the developmental level of the children and the large work books and supplementary material, games and activities are manageable for many of the partially sighted.

The teacher has a difficult task in attempting to understand the visually handicapped child's difficulties in terms of the cause and nature of the visual defect and the probable influence it has on the child's visual functioning. It is not possible at the present state of knowledge to tie up specific teaching approaches and adaptations of material to match precisely the problems arising from specific visual defects.

However, there are some approaches in presenting reading materials which have been found in the experience of teachers to be helpful in relation to specific difficulties in seeing.

Difficulties resulting from specific problems of sight For instance, pupils with a condition which affects the clarity of the area of central vision may be helped in reading by focusing their gaze just below the printed line rather than on it. Thus the top half of the letters which afford the most easily recognizable clues remain within the area of clearer vision. A child with this particular difficulty may also be helped by trailing a pencil or marker just below the line of print as he attempts to read it.

Some visually handicapped children may evidence low motivation towards using print, as a result of lack of encouragement or positive discouragement to use their sight for this purpose. Here again, the use of closed circuit television, the presentation of enlarged material on slide projectors, the use of flash cards, and language master machines which expose single words or short phrases from the reading book can help to concentrate attention. A simple exposure device in the form of a card covering the printed page with slit openings to reveal a controlled amount of text can also be used. Even the colour cue method of teaching reading such as *Words in Colour* (Gettegno, 1962) which at first sounds surprising as a teaching approach for children who do not see well, seems to help some pupils without

85

impaired colour vision to concentrate on material presented in print form.

In the case of adult partially sighted readers, Shaw (1969) observed that those with cataract were not helped so much by an increase in the size of print as by a slight increase in its boldness. Myopic subjects on the other hand found their reading facilitated by an increase in the size rather than in the weight of print but subjects suffering from glaucoma found that bold type was generally more helpful in their case. This study showed that an improvement of 35 per cent could be expected when the best features of typography were combined. The aspects exerting most influence on this improvement were size of type, which accounted for half of the improvement in legibility, increased boldness which added a quarter to the total factors of increased success, and finally a clear sans serif typeface which accounted for one eighth of the improvement noted.

Enlarged print The question of enlargement of print poses a different set of problems in the case of children with impaired vision from those to be considered in the case of partially sighted adults, the majority of whom are to be found in the middle and upper age groups. Children can bring their reading material close to the eye, thus affecting a spontaneous effect of enlargement since the lens is so flexible in its accommodation during this period of life. Over the years the possibility of discovering an 'optimum type' for school books has been considered by teachers, but no specific form or size of typeface has been found to be universally well suited to the needs of all visually handicapped pupils. A slightly bolder than average Gill Sans Serif or Plantin typeface has been recommended as a good working presentation by some teachers of the visually handicapped. Typeface should not be too heavy, since the characteristic spaces in letters can be somewhat occluded if the presentation is too bold in the pattern of printed letters and words.

Lighting, magnification, and position of work An experimental study has been followed up by a series of commentaries by Sykes (1975 and 1977). In total these give a comprehensive consideration of the question of print legibility for children with impaired vision. Comparing the effectiveness of standard print and enlarged print in facilitating reading skills he concludes that the use of large print in itself did little to help the young partially sighted reader but he suggests, as do most practising teachers, that attention should be given to the total layout of the print page in terms of the clear well-spaced presentation of material. Length of line and width of margin may also contribute to a well-displayed page. Attention is again drawn to the importance of appropriate illumination with a recommended level of fifty foot candles for low vision children who should be provided with portable reading lamps to permit regulation of intensity of light to suit their individual requirements. Photophobic children, such as albinos, will of course need to avoid glare and shiny light-reflective surfaces such as glossy pages and highly polished desk tops. The Department of Education and Science Bulletin No. 33 *Lighting in Schools* contains an appendix with particular reference to schools for the partially sighted, but questions of print presentation, illumination and teaching apparatus in reading should be considered for the visually handicapped pupil in any educational setting.

The position in which the reading material is placed also warrants attention. If the pupil needs to hold the material close to his eye, or if he uses a magnifier or low visual aid which necessitates a reduced focal length, his working position may give rise to tension or to bad posture unless care is taken to avoid this. If the reading book is placed on the flat surface of a desk or table top, the child may want to bend right over it in order to bring his gaze close enough to see it clearly thereby casting a shadow on to the page and adopting a stooped, cramped and uncomfortable position for reading and writing. A desk that is basically of the right size, and which has a sloping adjustable lid or the provision of a reading stand, can mitigate the difficulty of dealing with work at such close range.

The use of low vision aids or magnifiers can have some influence on the form of attack made on reading skills. A respected aim in promoting fluency in reading is one which emphasizes the ability to perceive words and phrases as wholes rather than concentrating on individual letters in succession. Visually handicapped children with a limited eye-span, or those using optical aids which only enable them to see one or two letters or part of a word at a time, may be expected to encounter problems with regard to fluency in reading. They can be helped by an approach which affords the opportunity for a period of word analysis followed by synthesis. However, Sykes (1977) in commenting on the child-centred approach to the teaching of reading which involves the learner in encountering written words from his own experience notes that the success of this method is dependent on the use of whole words, phrases and sentences. He draws attention to the fact that the phonic method which emphasizes the form and sound of individual letters and groups of letters, presents a more manageable task for some children with impaired sight, although fluency may be restricted because the analysis of words results in a slower rate of accomplishment. Thus it may be advisable to use either the whole-word method or the part method or even a combination of both according to the needs of the individual pupil; the possibility of introducing groups of letters notable for ease of visual recognition as well as frequency of use, is an interesting suggestion reminiscent of some of the teaching approaches in character recognition in braille.

Pre-reading activities Whatever form the visual handicap of the pupil manifests, the complex process of reading for him, as for other children, will be rooted in speaking and listening. As for all children his ability to develop meaningful language and converse is likely to be enhanced by listening to stories, re-telling them and acting them. An information sheet for parents issued by the John Aird School for the Partially Sighted (1975) suggests ways in which opportunities for these activities can be encouraged at home. Children who do not see well will require pre-reading books with bright simple attractive pictures. They will need to be helped to realize the difference between reading a story and telling a story and to understand that the written words, not simply the pictures, convey meaning. Their wish to use books may need to be awakened and the first books they use should be accessible, attractive, and of a manageable size for them to handle. Children's libraries in the neighbourhood are an excellent source of well-presented story books.

The beginning of writing Before the finer muscle movements involved in reading and writing are practised, the larger muscle movements need to be experienced and developed. Games involving imitative movements, including left-to-right movement of arms and hands, can easily be combined with practice in the spoken word. Nursery rhymes, singing games and action songs are important and enjoyable pre-reading activities for the visually handicapped child, who may need a good deal of free activity in gaining knowledge of the world around him before he begins to read and write about it.

These activities are a preparation for writing as well as for reading, since speaking, listening and movement are essential bases for this form of communication. It is both important that the child has something to write about, and that he develops the technical skills that enable him to do so. The technical skills can offer some problems to children with poor vision. Manipulation of materials, pattern matching and recognition are necessary pre-skills in this area for pupils whose view of a figure is blurred or fragmented.

For the visually handicapped child who needs to work at close range in painting, drawing and eventually in writing, small easels or even blackboards give him the opportunity to make big bold shapes involving the use of arm and hand in a free and uncramped position. Linked patterns of undulating lines help to develop the 'feel' of fluent movements before actual letter shapes are attempted.

Attention to handwriting and to typing The Marion Richardson scheme of teaching handwriting, growing out of patterns formed from letters is well suited to the visually handicapped in that the shape of the letters is represented and reinforced. Children who see poorly sometimes do not know where to start in the formation of a letter and a cursive rather than a separated script can be helpful to them. The use of closed circuit TV, enlarged material shown on a projector, or a close individual demonstration is necessary for such children who cannot easily see the process of drawing letter shapes. Practice in large movements making the shape of the letters and vocalizing the shapes and directions of movement may be needed before more conventional graphic forms are used.

Paper ruled with clear black lines give a guide to 'above' and 'below' line letter drawing. It can amuse and interest children to draw their attention to the characteristic letter shapes through describing them in terms of animation; the giraffe letters with their long necks above the line and the monkey letters with their tails curling below the line.

The use of a pencil which gives a heavy black line, and of felt tipped pens in clear bright colours enables the child to see for himself the shapes he has drawn and the letters which he has written. Both the thickness and the size of the written forms can be gradually diminished.

Using writing for names and labels, associating the written word with the person, the object, the action, is part of the beginning of written experiences. The difference between lower and upper case letters needs to be introduced carefully to avoid confusion.

The appearance of written work in a group of children with visual handicaps is likely to be very varied, from the minute style and tiny illustrations of some of the myopic pupils to the untidy apparently unco-ordinated attempts of some of the other pupils who find it difficult to reproduce a graphic shape. Every encouragement to write should be offered with the opportunities for the pupils to compile their own scrap books and story books.

It can be useful for the visually handicapped pupil to learn typewriting, since even with practice his handwriting may be relatively slow, and evidence his difficulty in keeping on a line. For examination purposes, typewriting is particularly useful. Nevertheless it does not replace handwriting as an art, and adequate time, and appropriate pre-writing activities and materials need to be employed in fostering this basic skill.

Teaching of mathematics and number concepts to visually handicapped pupils

Overcoming difficulties in basic mathematical concepts Inability to see shapes clearly, or perhaps at all, with consequently a reduced opportunity to be aware of number groups, such as a clump of five trees at the far end of a garden, or eight seagulls bobbing on the sea in the distance, means that children with severe levels of visual handicap have a less informative and less inviting background against which to develop an interest in mathematical concepts than would be the case for children whose vision is not impaired.

It might be expected that total lack of sight, in particular, would be likely to presuppose difficulty, or at least delay, in many areas involving an understanding of relationships in number, size, and shape, as well as in spatial concepts. Just as the child with little or no sight has lacked or has received diminished incidental experiences in seeing printed or written words displayed in slogans and advertisements in his everyday environment, so children with little or no sight are likely to have a limited experience of visual pattern and shape of the kind encountered by the fully sighted child in graphic and pictorial material as well as in the objects that surround him in his ordinary daily life. The round plate, the square table, the matching set of cutlery for each person at the table must be explored by the fingers or by the close gaze of the visually handicapped youngster. Not only in infancy, but as he is growing up too, his deprivation of the clear visual experience of form and shape may put him at some disadvantage compared with the fully sighted pupil. Even in the secondary school state Thwaites (1970) refers to the ways in which the visual stimuli of modern architecture and industrial design impinge on the minds of seeing children, and draw attention to the mathematical concepts at or near the root of the understanding of these forms.

The child who sees little or nothing will therefore not only need to explore and to discover the characteristics of shapes through tactile investigation, he will also need to build up a vocabulary of meaningful terms through which to express the result of his discoveries. Such words as vertex, edge, face and curve must be linked with tangible examples that evidence the characteristics which the terms embody. As the discoveries become more complex, so does the need for relevant vocabulary increase. Beginning with reference to shape and continuing with the critical features of shapes, a growing store of words to describe terms of weight, measurement, and amount is necessary. Reinforcement by tangible or, for children with some vision, by pictorial evidence of relationships is essential. The idea of fractions, for example, can be conveyed by halving and quartering stiff pieces of paper and giving names to the wholes and parts. The learning of number bonds from 0 to 20 can begin with tangibles and as an increasing understanding develops, the need for tactile verification will diminish.

In the case of the child using his vision, examples of objects that he can explore in tactile terms should be brought into a position for attentive gaze also. Eventually, attention must be given to ways of recording mathematical data that are appropriate for the child's level of seeing; but recording should follow a developing understanding of relationships and an increasing comprehension of shape and pattern gained through first-hand exploration. In short, the visually handicapped child, like the seeing child, should be helped to think mathematically, not simply to record symbols on one or more of the many ingeniously adapted pieces of apparatus available to him.

Nevertheless, the ability to transfer a visual problem into terms of symbols and equations, as well as the development of logical thinking and spatial sense are considered by Wilson (1968) necessary attributes for the pupil to be successful in mathematics. In the days when rather formal teaching of mathematics was current, it was optimistically stated in the *Handbook for School Teachers of the Blind* (College of Teachers of the Blind, 1956), that there were no difficulties inherent in the subject of mathematics itself which could not be overcome by blind pupils. The realistic teacher, however, will recognize that there are difficulties, particularly for the congenitally and totally blind child, both in the presentation of material and in the subsequent processes of understanding and recording results, but that these difficulties present challenges which do not prevent this subject from being a vital and interesting one in which high levels of success can eventually be obtained by some pupils.

Fortunately, many of the problems arising in the teaching of mathematics have been energetically tackled by teachers who, mindful of the limited experience of blind children, have developed and adapted concrete material in graded schemes of work to provide learning situations appropriate to the child's level of understanding.

In order to use these situations as effectively as possible, a good deal of discussion relating to the objects handled, as well as plenty of opportunity for tactile investigation and manipulation is required before the pupils are ready to collect data as a result of counting and sorting items. Beginning at a simple level the pupils are lead into the mastery of different ways of recording and representing mathematical problems and their solutions through increasingly complex stages. The attempts at recording should be introduced gradually as the idea of pattern and relationship develops, so that what is symbolized is understood, and the whole process of developing mathematical concepts is tied in with vital activity. As experience and understanding increase, more formal and more abstract work can be introduced, with problems posed, and solutions worked out with a decreasing need to refer to concrete examples.

Play activities leading to number work   Initially it is through play that objects are handled and examined, with colourful and visually attractive shapes giving as much invitation as possible to the child with a little vision to use it in increasing his sensory experience and fuelling his curiosity. Play, which begins at home and côntinues without much noticeable break into the early school years, can offer ways of helping the visually handicapped child to appreciate the code of relationships which underlies essential mathematical concepts. This view is put forward by Tooze (1967) in describing play situations in which the visually handicapped infant is led into discovering that some things are smaller than others, some heavier than others, and eventually that objects can be grouped into the patterns that we call numbers. Thus the beginning of basic number concept coincides well with an active play situation; it is important, however, to ensure that the material used is both manageable and distinctive in tactile terms, as well as colourful for children with some sight.

The building up of a programme involving an increasing awareness of numbers, shapes, and patterns should be an enjoyable exercise for both teacher and pupils. Many of the activities relate well to familiar play or domestic situations. The principle of one-to-one correspondence can be demonstrated by putting an egg in each egg cup when setting a table, then a knife by each plate. The idea of sets is now developing.

Sets and number relationships   Indeed in most children the idea of sets begins to develop intuitively as they start collecting things together, and progress as they sort objects out into collections with particular characteristics. The attention of the visually handicapped child may need to be drawn quite specifically to these characteristics. If a child meets several sets, in which the members of any one set can be matched one-to-one with those of any other, then this collection of sets possesses an abstract quality which is the cardinal number of the sets. Gradually the child becomes aware that different sets can have different numbers of elements, and this realization is related to the development of the concept of ordinal numbers. If sets are arranged in the order of an increasing number of elements (seriation) each set containing one more than its predecessor, the concepts of cardination and ordination are coming together. The difficulty for some visually handicapped children is that they are unlikely to be able to take in at a glance the information with which they are presented.

Sometimes ingenuity is needed in order to demonstrate a principle. Seriation can be evidenced in a tactile way through the use of nesting shapes and the handling and arrangement in graduating size of dolls or toy animals. Classification involving the mixture of two discrete elements can be introduced in terms of shape and texture, for instance in using six bricks of the same size, some of which are smooth, and some roughly textured. The contents of a box of mixed objects can be sorted, classified, and counted, with the groups of similar and then of identical objects totalled and compared. Equalization of groups can be demonstrated by dividing a pile of sweets exactly into two boxes.

Size, shape, capacity and volume   The beginning of an understanding of capacity and volume should have been forming as a result of such activities as sand and water play, with the filling and emptying of containers of different sizes. Simple comparison of lengths can be shown by the child measuring different fingers and book and desk lengths, but these activities are really quite difficult for a blind child and require practice from him as well as patience from his teacher. Games and activities which can help the visually handicapped child to sort and classify, according to a number of criteria, such as shape, size, and texture, can be started without the use of symbolic representation, and then lead into its use.

Adaptations in learning materials and in methods of presentation   Although many of the activities described appear comparable to those undertaken by fully sighted children, the teacher with a visually handicapped child or a group of such children in the class will need to give particular attention to some aspects of the work. In devising and selecting the material for activities, the teacher must bear in mind not only the goal of the activity, but its manageability in terms of the child who sees little or nothing. Control of material is more difficult for the visually handicapped child to achieve than for the fully sighted. Plastic containers or compartmental boxes can be used to hold small objects and units of material. Time can be wasted and confusion can ensue if pieces of material skid off the top of the desk or table while they are being handled, and it is essential that tactile materials should not only be accessible to the visually handicapped child, but also capable of thorough exploration by him. For example, although buttons and small objects can be mounted on cards for matching numbers, objects should in general be presented in the early stages in such a way that they can be explored in all dimensions. The length of the sessions spent on specific activities warrants attention also. Some visually handicapped children can become bored and distractable whilst undertaking sorting and classifying activities if they are expected to continue doing so for too long at one time. These pupils need enough time to complete tasks, to explore and to investigate, but a new activity leading to a new concept should be introduced as soon as the pupil is ready for it. The goals which form the objective of each activity should be clearly set, and the progression of activities matched to the developing capacities of the child's thinking. The teacher will need to keep a record of each individual pupil's progress, and to be alert to adapt any activities with which the child is having difficulties as a result of his sight defect.

Recording of work   Gradually the sets of facts discovered as a result of investigation and discussion can be recorded in a variety of ways, through speech, and later through permanent symbolic representation. Representation can be very simple at first, using pegboards or wooden blocks, with the introduction of braille or print numerical and operational symbols as the pupil begins to understand the principles represented. Histograms offer an effective way of beginning to use one object to represent several, and to show the early stages of collecting, sorting, and comparing data.

With regard to the progression of activities and the appropriate stages of introducing various types of recording in the primary school, reference can most usefully be made to the lively scheme of work for blind children described by F. H. G. Tooze (1967). The way in which this approach emphasizes the structuring of situations to enable the individual to make discoveries for himself does not preclude group work and the introduction of some formal learning, but it does emphasize the value of ensuring that the pupil understands procedures rather than simply repeating them, but the use of an organized system of number materials should be adopted.

Tooze suggests that, after the early play activities of the type described above, the use of colour factor rods should be introduced when the children are about six. A magnetized backing can be given to the blocks which can then be used on a steel plate to retain their position. Dienes logic blocks and multi-base arithmetic blocks or Stern's apparatus can be used effectively with visually handicapped pupils also, although the blocks are somewhat less easy for those without sight to handle. Here again, it is important for the pupils to understand what the blocks are representing. The caveat which Dearden (1969) puts forward about the use of discovery methods in the early stages of mathematics teaching with sighted children has, if anything, even more significance in the case of the visually handicapped. His questions as to why wooden blocks should be seen as a concrete analogue of mathematical relationships if the pupil is not taught something of those relationships is even more cogent in the case of pupils who see poorly or who do not see at all. For these children especially, initiation must be undertaken in order to learn about concepts which are exemplified by concrete objects and the arrangement of representational forms.

Another form of representation which some blind children will be ready to use by this stage is the cubarithm board. This apparatus consists of a small, firm plastic board with lines of square apertures in which metal cubes can be fitted as required for recording or for working sums. These small cubes bear braille numerical and operational signs on each of their facets. Detailed instructions with regard to the use of the cubarithm board as well as suggestions as to the advantages and disadvantages of its use are given in *The Teaching of Science and Mathematics to the Blind*. In this, F. H. G. Tooze suggests a graduation of tasks of increasing complexity leading to the application of the four rules and of learned tables. The more formal approach is introduced when colour factor blocks are used for setting out and solving a problem and then the result is recorded by means of braille numerical symbols made on the Perkins braille upward writer. Side by side with the pupil's own attempts at recording work, brailled or clearly printed work cards can be introduced. These are useful in providing problems for pupils to solve at different levels of competence and understanding of mathematical thinking. In compiling such cards, clarity of content and presentation are essential.

Some of the pupils, including the totally blind, will be able to record work without much difficulty by using the Perkins upward writer when they are about 8 years old, although complete severance from the concrete will not have taken place in that colour factor blocks and the cubarithm board may still be used in the working out stages of a problem. Motivation in areas involving the four rules can be heightened and concepts reinforced by the pupils themselves making pictographs. The understanding of sequence and of number relationships can be shown by reference to the number line which is composed of linked units marked off with braille symbols; children will vary in their need to refer to such concrete evidence as a check during the processes of calculation. Indeed references to activities in mathematics as in other areas of learning for visually handicapped children should be considered as a guide line if suggested age-groups are quoted, since pupils are likely to span a range with regard to their readiness in understanding concepts. Tobin's study of the conservation of substance (1972b) shows this to be an important factor.

When the pupils are ready for a further form of representation in number work, the Cranmer abacus can be introduced. This is an adaptation of the Japanese abacus and works on a base of five. It is light and portable and the beads are easy to handle but do not slip about with the result that some pupils become very quick and adept in its use. Davidow (1966) gives a detailed but clear exposition of its use in full, but F. H. G. Tooze recommends it for addition and subtraction rather than for multiplication and division. He also suggests that in the later stages of the primary school pupils should construct three-dimensional forms such as the tetrahedron for themselves. Work of this kind involves the child in a disciplined study of shape including the investigation of edges and faces, thus giving direction and conclusion to earlier play with shapes. At the same stage and alongside this practical work increasing opportunities for recording the wording and solution of problems should be attempted. The cubarithm board and the abacus may still be used with something of the function of the pencil and notebook which the sighted child uses for jotting down interim stages of working. The use of the Taylor frame, another piece of specialized apparatus fulfilling a comparable role, is now seldom taught especially at primary school level. The ingenious but elusive small metal rods known as Taylor type are difficult for younger children to handle and involve the learning of an additional series of numerical and later of algebraic symbols.

The increasing availability and subsequently the universal usage of the Perkins upward writer which enables the braille symbols to be embossed on to paper, has diminished the need for using the Taylor frame, and enabled pupils to check their own work more easily. However, even now there is not a unanimous point of view throughout the schools with regard to the setting out of mathematical working in braille, and even a mathematical code which includes all operational, numerical and algebraic symbols has been subject to revisions and alterations that are not always adopted in practice.

Some teachers prefer a method of layout for mathematics in braille which follows as closely as possible to that used in printed forms, thus involving some vertical setting out in the process of working. Whittaker (1967) however, has devised a method of layout and working which has been referred to as the linear method. The figures and operational signs are set out along the line in horizontal form, and it is claimed that this minimizes the need for manipulating the Perkins by placing figures underneath each other. Whilst merit can be found in either of these approaches, teachers of blind pupils at secondary level are presented with a challenging task in dealing with a group of pupils who have come into a secondary class from different primary schools or departments using different forms of mathematical layout.

Mathematics for the secondary school pupil   Sims's (1967) studies of the teaching of mathematics to academically able pupils at the secondary school stage, show that the most evident differences between them and sighted pupils of comparable age and ability was that the speed of calculation that could be expected from the blind pupils was slower, except in the case of mental arithmetic. The blind pupils in her experience had greater difficulty both in comprehending and in replicating diagrammatic work. She also considered that logical thinking was less evident than the result of repetitive learning in the case of the blind pupils.

Despite such problems, blind pupils of good ability have, with the help of skilled teachers, been able to achieve high levels of success in mathematics. The syllabus leading to external examinations at both GCE 'O' and 'A' Levels as well as the CSE, can be followed with adaptations in the presentation and recording of material, even with the use of a 'talking computer', but with the examination content the same as for the fully sighted pupil. The value of the subject must not be under-estimated in terms not only of developing logical thinking and problem solving, but also in terms of opening up vocational possibilities and forming an essential skill in many areas of daily life. An understanding of the binary system, for instance, may be required in computer studies which are undertaken by some blind pupils at sixth-form level.

For the pupils who find abstract thinking difficult, opportunities for tactile discovery, comparison and reference should not cease at the end of primary school, since some blind pupils even at adolescence may show deficiencies both in the characteristics of objects and in spatial awareness. The need for pupils to be able to manage their own money, to plan ahead in terms of cause and effect, to budget and keep simple accounts is self-evident. Basic mathematical skills may have to be continued in the area of 'social arithmetic' throughout the secondary school years for some pupils who will need carefully graduated schemes and work assignments involving practical activities of weighing, measuring, and counting. Project and group work offers a useful opportunity to involve pupils in activities including construction and calculation.

Using residual vision for mathematics The pupil who has useful vision should be encouraged to use this purposefully in his work in mathematics, although he should not be inhibited from tactile exploration and the use of concrete material which helps to clarify

99

concepts. Suitable commercially produced material abounds in which clear diagrammatic representation and graded materials are available with teaching guidelines, pupils' workbooks and workcards. The material in such schemes is generally presented under broad topic headings which indicate the logical sequence of the work presented. Visually handicapped pupils relying on their vision may need plenty of practice at each stage and the general recommendations with regard to the position of work, lighting and demonstration of processes, even to enlarged drawing of geometrical figures and algebraic signs should be observed as for teaching of writing. Tables such as logarithms have been produced in large print form since the standard form presents so dense a page of figures.

In schools for sighted children there have been moves to replace logarithms by slide rules up to CSE and GCE 'O' Level Mathematics. Now the pocket electronic calculator looks like making both of these aids to calculation archaic at school level. The implications of this for the teaching of mathematics are hard to predict. In the case of visually handicapped pupils attention must be directed towards the development and production of instruments with an output that they can either read or hear.

Clear pictorial representation is well suited to pupils with enough vision to make use of this form of presentation. Data can be presented pictorially in such a way that attention is drawn to relationships that might otherwise be less clearly shown by a mass of numerals. A scheme which emphasizes the presentation of data in pictorial form, at the same time giving attention to the building up of a meaningful vocabulary of mathematical terms, is described by Lovatt (1970). He uses the Nuffield mathematics approach in work for educationally subnormal pupils, but the clarity of the presentation and the emphasis on simple graphical representation make this an approach that would be of value to less academic partially sighted pupils. A further advantage of such a scheme is that the individual and small group situations needed for a class of pupils of mixed ability and mixed visual competence would find in it work well suited to individual levels.

The Schools Council 'Look and Think' Project may have implications for the learning of mathematics by pupils with some vision, since its emphasis on shape discrimination, attention to critical features, and to symmetry and perspective, offer at least the possibility of transfer to situations involving the mathematical concepts of such phenomena as shape, pattern, and sequence.

If a secure basis of experience and discussion with plenty of opportunity for practice is given to blind and partially sighted pupils during their primary school years, their secondary school programme in mathematics can approximate in content at least to that of fully sighted pupils of comparable ability. Teachers of blind and partially sighted pupils still confer in attempts to resolve some of the problems regarding suitable content and appropriate recording that still await solution, but the importance of mathematics presented at a level appropriate to the needs and abilities of visually handicapped pupils can be doubted by none.

Mobility orientation and movement training

Value of physical activities including sports The thud of a large soft ball on a bat can be heard as a team of blind boys, some totally without sight, enjoy their game of cricket on an eighteen foot grass pitch. A spectator would note some adaptations to the traditional game; one bounce of the ball before a catch being allowed to those who do not see at all, and the ball itself, made of white plastic and containing a handful of swirling roller bearings needs to be heard by the players. According to Raffle (1970) who enjoyed such games at school and later encouraged visually handicapped students to try it, one of the few drawbacks occurred when the equivalent of 'bad light' flew overhead or traffic noise at the bottom of the lawn masked the sound of the ball. The purpose of the game was exactly the same as for sighted boys – enjoyment.

Another sight that can surprise the visitor to a school for the blind is that of the pupils running flat out in track events, swimming and diving to competition levels, or spending leisure hours practising judo, wrestling or rowing. Schools for the partially sighted can also present an impressive list of the physical recreation activities which many of their pupils take up; the pursuits described by one school as being part of their programme included horse-riding, hill-walking, swimming in river and sea, canoeing in river and sea, rock-climbing and rifle shooting. There is a particular value in the sports and pursuits that a visually handicapped pupil will wish to continue after leaving school, both from the point of view of maintaining fitness, and making social contacts with people of similar interests. Consequently, it is undesirable that physical education and games times should be used by the visually handicapped child attending ordinary school as a time to have 'coaching' in work that he has found difficult to follow in academic lessons. The times of the day or week given to active participation in sport and physical activities are not expendable, and individual programmes need to be worked out for the visually handicapped pupil who cannot or does not wish to take part in team events.

Undue fears that the visually handicapped child may be in danger of damaging his sight futher, particularly as a result of retinal detachment, are less frequently encountered than in the past, and if medical advice is sought and observed, activities can be adapted even for those few children considered to be at risk.

Early activities to develop purposeful movement   Easy and purposeful movement is not achieved however, by every visually handicapped pupil; early encouragement and opportunities to explore the physical environment together with training in orientation are necessary precursors to later achievement, and children deprived of these opportunities are likely to have difficulties in independent mobility later on.

Both the blind and the partially sighted child in his early primary school years will need the same large muscle and co-ordinating physical activities as the fully sighted child. Games which also include rhythmic movement such as clapping, skipping, and hopping are especially enjoyable. Interpretative movement can be difficult since demonstration cannot be seen or cannot be seen well, but action learning and kinaesthetic demonstration can help the children in animal games which include rabbit hops or duck waddles. Active outdoor play will provide opportunities for crawling and climbing but adult intervention to encourage and motivate this may be needed as the trees, blocks and tunnels of an adventure playground if not seen will be less inviting to spontaneous exploration!

Consequently, movement training for the young primary school child who sees little or nothing will need to be based on body awareness, movement in space, and movement that relates to objects and people. He needs to develop a knowledge and control of his arms, legs and body, and in exploring rather than shunning his physical environment he will gain experience in finding out what happens when he attempts to move himself about in relation to objects. Purposeful movement has to be developed according to the demands of a situation, so the visually handicapped child will need to move in as many different ways and in as many different situations as possible when his courage and initiative increase. Such activities will help him to develop awareness of the position of his trunk, head and limbs in space, both when still and in movement, increasing his ability to maintain balance, and developing his kinaesthetic or 'muscle-memory'.

Using all the senses in movement training Without the co-ordinating sense of sight, the blind child, and especially the congenitally blind child, may show inept and uncontrolled movement; he may also fear space, and lacking a sense of direction, be unaware of directional change as well as being unable to correct or replicate a movement. In such cases there is clearly a need for timely and individual remedial work. D. Tooze (1967) traces such delays in readiness for purposeful movement to apprehension as a result of early limitations in the opportunity to play and explore actively. She considers that primary school work must lay emphasis on specific training in using the senses of hearing, touch and smell as cues in helping to develop orientation. Response to sound cues may be practised in chanting games, in following the sound of the teacher's voice and in games with large cane bell-balls that are easy to follow and to handle. The attention of the pupils can be drawn to the use of reflected sounds as a cue since some blind children will instinctively clap their hands or click their tongues when approaching a wall and the ability to respond to these cues can be improved with practice. Both Leonard (1967) and D. Tooze (1972) refer to the necessity for visually handicapped children to use their senses in an unusual manner – playing attention to the information gathered through the senses to an extent which the sighted child need not do. In locating places, for example, some shops notably a baker's or a fishmonger's, can be recognized by smell, as can the school dining-room. There are surface cues also, which can be noted and talked about, small slopes and changes in gradient, even within the school campus, about which the pupil can be alerted to feel the difference in weight and effort in moving up or down hill. A heightened awareness of the environment, and an increased ability to use many different sources of information when moving about will help to give a sound basis of training before formal mobility work begins.

Development of physical co-ordination and body awareness Sensitivity both to the developmental readiness and the individual techniques which each child will develop is essential if an effective sequence of exercises concentrating on body image, laterality and directionality is to be practised. In working out such programmes the screening test devised by Cratty and Sammes (1968) shows the extent to which the pupil can identify the parts of his body, the planes of his body (side, back, front, etc.) and left and right directionality. The progression of work from body-image training, through dynamic spatial orientation, to map-reading and mobility is outlined clearly by these authors. Carrying out verbal instructions with regard to bodily movement can be quite difficult for a blind child, and it is important that the instructions are clear and also that they are meaningful to him. Kooyman (1967) believes communication to be a fundamental aspect of physical education for pupils with defective vision. The relationship between the 'ego' and the external world is not easy for the blind child to establish, since he is likely to have less information, less control, less co-ordination and less stimulation than the non-handicapped child. He must develop an adequate and trustworthy relationship with his environment through movement, but his body may seem less useful, less at his disposal, than that of a sighted child, even seeming at times to be an obstacle rather than a means of expression. However the self-realization that can grow from meaningful communication and purposeful movement can be strengthened in active play and in mastery of the physical self.

Mobility as a school subject Mobility has by now come to be considered as an essential school subject for blind children culminating in their ability to walk through familiar and unfamiliar environments self-dependently. The necessary competence can be broken down into sub-skills and taught to pupils in the same way as other school subjects. During the 1950s and 1960s both researchers and teachers in Great Britain became interested in the technique of using the long cane which had been so successful in the USA especially in the rehabilitation of war-blinded veterans. La Duke, an American expert in mobility, initiated work in which two Liverpool schools for the blind were involved and in 1968 a special training centre for instructors was established now known as the National Mobility Centre. School teachers as well as social workers began to undertake this highly specific training in which a chest-high white stick is used in a series of sweeping movements to detect kerbs and obstacles. But the new techniques offered much more than that. The training was highly technical with its own terminology, such as 'lining up' and 'squaring off' being used to describe alignment and turning away from a fixture. Efficient ways of moving about indoors as well as out-of-doors were taught, including opening doors, locating chairs and tables, even retrieving lost objects from the floor with maximum safety.

Teachers, however, were increasingly convinced that the use of any mobility aid, especially one as useful as the long cane, could only be acceptable if training in its use was the culmination of a more basic course in orientation and movement training. The difficulty of time-tabling mobility with its need for regular individual instruction as well as practical sessions frequently outside the school campus was tackled in a series of conferences whose recommendations are published under the title *Mobility Training in Schools for the Visually Handicapped* (College of Teachers of the Blind, 1971).

In order to render such training programmes manageable Shannon (1971) suggests that an appropriately trained teacher should not only be responsible for the training of individual pupils, but a workshop project carefully developed whereby other teachers and house-staff can be instructed in pre-cane skills. Practical sessions using the blindfold with discussions to clarify and solve problems can be undertaken. Stress is constantly given to the necessity for early attention to body awareness, posture and gait before formal training in cane techniques. Directional techniques, protective techniques, familiarization with the environment and the use of a sighted guide follow this basic training.

Maps and diagrams in mobility training   The interpretation of tactile maps and diagrams in terms of orientation form a key feature of an effective mobility course. The pupil can be taught to plot his own chart with mapping pins as he recognizes landmarks and works out his direction of travel. Both research and practice have been directed towards co-ordination in the use of symbols in map-reading.

The question of standardization of design and symbolization in tactile route maps for the blind is analysed by James and Campbell (1975). They classify important landmarks under the headings of line symbols, point symbols, and texture symbols. The first group of these indicates such features as guiding surfaces, railings, walls and footpaths to the blind traveller, whilst the point symbols show the presence of possible obstacles or hazards, crossing points, and facilities such as telephone boxes. The last group of symbols gives information on the quality of surface under foot, the presence of parks, woods and grass verges. Questions of scale, coding space, information density and distinguishability are considered, together with the prime need to exchange information between all those concerned with the production of embossed maps, so that standardization is achieved in the way that information is presented.

Training in directionality and in tactile discrimination underlies the successful use of these presentations; it must also be concerned with demonstration and practice in the movements involved in handling the long cane.

Parental involvement in training schemes Parental involvement in mobility training has been a challenging development in some schools for the blind. At Tapton Mount School, Sheffield, for example, parents are trained by a mobility teacher from the school; their experiences under the blindfold as they negotiate foot and public transport journeys, walk along crowded pavements and weave through busy shops give them an increased and realistic understanding of the demands of mobility for the visually handicapped child. In addition, parental interest in this key area of training is likely to ensure that mobility practice undertaken by the pupil at school does not lapse during holiday times. Ideally this parents' programme should begin before the child comes to school, continuing through active play and pursuits which encourage freedom of movement throughout his school years and culminating in the formal mobility exercises involved in long-cane usage.

Mannerisms in visually handicapped children   Attention is given in the Vernon Report (1972) to the necessity for mobility training and the attempt to diminish mannerisms. Fine (1968) had drawn attention to the prevalence of mannerisms and poor mobility in her Survey of Blind and Partially Sighted Pupils in England and Wales. In this she recorded that 9·6 per cent of the partially sighted and 45 per cent of the blind displayed one or more mannerisms. Poor mobility which could not be ascribed to physical handicap was encountered in 4·5 per cent of the partially sighted and 25 per cent of the blind. Recent evidence (Jastrzembska, 1974) shows that there are some pointers which indicate that eye-poking is related more directly to visual impairment than other mannerisms such as rocking which is more likely to be associated with somatosensory deprivation.

Mobility training for children with partial vision   Nevertheless the observations in the Vernon Report (1972) with regard to partially sighted children show that their needs must not be ignored. The percentages of partially sighted children affected both by mannerisms and by poor mobility were not insignificant even though they were predictably less than in the case of children considered educationally blind.

The movement training and mobility skills required by children with enough vision to be considered as partially sighted has been less clearly defined both in research and in practical teaching programmes than the carefully structured training schemes for those who are considered to be dependent on their other senses rather than that of sight. This is emphasized by the use of the blindfold as a normal aspect of training procedure in mobility.

The individual differences in the way in which partially sighted children and children with residual vision see means that each child will have a slightly different problem with regard to the extent and clarity of his visual panorama. Early training in body awareness and the relationship of the body to objects and its position in space is necessary, and specific training to help the child to make maximum use of his unimpaired senses by giving attention to cues transmitted by sound, touch, smell and kinaesthetic sensation can help him to locate and make use of directional information.

Dugmore (1973) gives examples of ways in which mobility training for partially sighted pupils ensures the opportunity for them to make the type of journey involved in going to work by public transport. This is essential practice in a residential school, but in many day-schools for the partially sighted pupils arrive by taxi or school bus and may not have had the chance to work out methods of independent travel in practical terms. Dugmore's scheme does more than simply expect the pupils to undertake public transport journeys of increasing difficulty. Tasks involving recognition of landmarks are set, problems encountered on the journey discussed later with teachers, and a methodical approach to overcoming difficulties is worked out with each pupil on an individual basis.

Specialized maps for partially sighted students have been developed and tested by Greenberg (1969) using white lines on a dark grey background; they were found to be useful to most of the pupils who attempted to use them.

Visually handicapped children in varied educational settings Pupils in ordinary schools who are visually handicapped, blind and partially sighted pupils attending schools for the mentally and physically handicapped may need training in mobility too. It can be all too easy for them to depend on fully sighted friends for getting about, and to be left out of team games in sports because they are not good at them or do not want to take part. Much of the normal work in a physical education programme can be of benefit to them but some of their needs in this respect are specialized and require the help of an advisory teacher for the visually handicapped.

On leaving school or further education it should be possible for the visually handicapped young person to choose whether or not he needs a mobility aid. If he does, there is a series of aids available to him. The long-cane for the use of which he should have received basic training while at school; the sonic torch – a rubber torch-shaped device which emits signals indicating the position of obstacles; sonic spectacles which consist of a head-mounted device working on a similar principle; finally a guide dog who will provide a companionable means of independent mobility. But whichever means he chooses, the basic education he has received in mobility and movement training will be invaluable.

Self-help skills

Daily living skills Breakfast time for most of us means taking the top off an egg, eating the egg with a small spoon, buttering toast, pouring out a cup of tea or coffee, adding just enough milk and one or two teaspoonfuls of sugar. What happens if we attempt to do all this under a blindfold? We are not in the same situation as the congenitally blind child who has never possessed vision nor the child with some sight, but this learning situation into which we can temporarily place ourselves highlights the necessity for giving practical training in the self-help skills of daily living to visually handicapped children by making us aware of the perceptual tasks involved in judging distances, balancing a weighted spoon, pouring liquids and locating objects without the guiding and co-ordinating sense of sight.

Training in social competence involves more than teaching the techniques leading to the mastery of such routine daily events as dressing, eating or finding and looking after one's belongings, but a reasonable level of adroitness in managing these skills can lessen the strain and anxiety for both the visually handicapped and the fully sighted since the sighted sometimes appear to be the ones who are ill at ease when a blind or partially sighted person puts salt into his tea or comes to work wearing a different coloured shoe on each foot. The opening-up of educational and vocational opportunities for the visually handicapped heightens the necessity for acceptable levels of personal appearance and the management of self-help skills. At the same time increasing emphasis on academic attainment as a passport to interesting jobs and tertiary education puts pressure on the time and energy of the blind and partially sighted pupil. Difficulties in managing routine social skills are likely to have been exacerbated if the visually handicapped child has been discouraged from doing things for himself at home or has spent years in an institutional atmosphere where many of his daily needs are catered for without effort or physical contribution being expected from him.

Training in personal independence Most schools for the visually handicapped do give attention to training in self-help skills (Childs, 1974) and many have worked out training in which both teachers and child care staff are involved. But if training in self-help skills begins when the visually handicapped child first comes to school it is already late, since the pre-school years embody the stages of perceptuo-motor development underlying the ability to perform simple tasks such as grasping, pouring liquids or lifting objects.

The school can face a diversity of problems when attempting to meet the needs of individual children in this area of training. The extent to which children have been encouraged to be independent in such matters at home will vary and some children will have had periods of illness or of being in hospital which may have emphasized their dependence; differences in the amount of vision and the way in which it is used may call for adaptations in the way some of the tasks are taught and undertaken; differences in the degree of developmental readiness will require the presentation of materials at the child's developmental rather than his chronological age. Finally, the ethos of the class or school will need to be such that training in self-help skills is considered vital, interesting and rewarding, not an unimportant 'extra' relegated to odd times and places so that it does not take time from more exciting subjects.

Systematic teaching is essential here although the child will need plenty of opportunities to find out for himself how to do things and to do them the way that suits him best, as well as having guided help in mastering techniques. A structured approach involving graded tasks of increasing difficulty and complexity can be undertaken. Simple activities such as spreading slices with butter and pouring milk into a cup are diversified until simple meals can be prepared and served. Eventually, in the last years at school, full meals can be undertaken with the necessary shopping, budgeting, and attention to nutrition forming part of the educational content. Cleaning and looking after a flat, laundering clothes, washing and making menus for a week, make such an essential course in domestic economy sound very like that undertaken by ordinary pupils at a comprehensive school. The end is the same but the means by which the pupils achieve these ends involve some adaptations in method, a few adaptations of equipment and systematic teaching in small groups or on an individual basis.

Graded checklists of skills An attempt to relate the performance of specific day-to-day tasks to appropriate ages in the case of blind children has been made in the Netherlands by Van der Zwan and Heslinga (1970). It is stressed, however, that this checklist should not be considered as a test scale but rather as a means of enabling teachers to note, methodically, whether or not there are gaps in the ability of their blind pupils to perform self-help skills which it would be reasonable to consider within the competence of a blind child of a given age. The seven categories covered in this 'checklist' relate to eating, dressing, personal grooming, orientation, communication, household skills, and a final section headed 'miscellaneous' concerned with items such as using keys, putting a plug into a socket, packing a suitcase and wrapping up a parcel. Much of this training is scheduled to take place in the primary school years, and in the Dutch situation is carried out by specially trained youth leaders who have charge of the residential and leisure aspects of the pupil's school life. The emphasis is on learning through doing and the pupils are encouraged to take part in a variety of domestic activities such as cooking, doing small repairs under supervision, choosing and taking care of their clothes.

Analysis of tasks Children with little or no sight find that the imitation of processes is difficult, so that even comparatively simple tasks taken for granted by the fully sighted will need to be analysed and broken down into manageable sub-skills. For example, in learning to pour out liquids it is necessary to place the receptacle on a flat surface, then the spout of the pouring vessel must be placed on the rim of the receptacle; both hands are used for this task, with one supporting the pouring vessel and the finger and thumb of the other hand steadying and controlling the spout of the vessel while the liquid is being poured. Another simple action, common to most meal times, involves holding a spoon steadily when it is full and being moved from the plate or bowl to the mouth; this action can be practised with a basin full of sand with attention being directed to the difference in weight when the spoon is full or empty.

A residential environment should give opportunity for systematic attention to this kind of training and the child-care staff have a major contribution to make here. Ideally, of course, much of this training should take place at home but parents themselves may need help in knowing how to tackle the problems involved. The short length of the school day may make it difficult to include such work in a day school and the severely visually handicapped child in an ordinary school or one for other handicaps may be in a situation where his need for specific training in these skills is not realized or understood.

Home economics Some of these skills can be dovetailed into a cookery and home economics programme. Simple cookery is a useful subject for blind and partially sighted children in the primary school since it is exciting and involves procedures of weighing, measuring, and attention to shapes and textures. If all goes well, it even has a consumable end product.

Groups will need to be small, since vigilance is needed to avoid accidents, and demonstration may be needed on an individual basis. Visually handicapped pupils will need time to find their way round the working room, locate equipment, learn to store materials in an orderly way and be alerted to any safety hazards such as power points and electrical equipment.

Visually handicapped pupils at secondary school level can undertake a home economics programme whose content is much the same as that for sighted pupils. Basic preparation techniques in cooking include rubbing in, mixing, beating, baking, and grilling, but not frying which is hazardous for those who do not see well. Commercial apparatus can be carefully chosen to help to minimize the practical difficulties of not seeing well, for instance a split-level cooker with eye-level grill, use of standard pinging electric timers and light brightly coloured plastic containers is recommended. The Disabled Living Foundation has listed apparatus and equipment especially useful for the partially sighted housewife and most of this is equally so for the pupil or student. Special equipment such as tea dispensers and milk savers can be obtained from the Royal National Institute for the Blind. Both gas and electric cookers can be fitted with braille markings. Teachers of domestic science in schools for the blind shared their ideas in adapting methods, for instance, in using homely measures such as teacups for measuring, (Chapman, 1970). Blind or poorly sighted pupils can be helped to use senses other than sight in locating and identifying ingredients. When containers are shaken, heavy syrup will sound different from a less viscous liquid such as vinegar. Smell, texture and weight all afford clues as to what a jar contains.

Techniques for visually limited pupils

In this, as in other areas of learning, the pupil with some vision can be helped to use it as effectively as possible. Demonstration of tasks such as peeling a potato may have to be undertaken in small groups, even individually, so that the pupil can see the action of the hands and the knife. Closed circuit television can be a useful means of clarifying difficult or complex procedures of a practical nature. The workroom will need to be appropriately lit, shining light-reflective surfaces are best avoided. Labelling of equipment, cupboards and their contents should be done clearly with a black felt-tipped pen. Personal grooming and choice and care of clothes as well as the aspects of cleaning and maintenance of equipment should be embodied in an up-to-date housecraft course. A small but useful literature has grown relating to the teaching of these subjects to visually handicapped pupils which includes *Overcoming Handicap* (Hedley, 1972). Recipe books and books on housecraft have been transcribed into braille but the teacher will find it practical to use plastic cards with braille or clearly printed recipes as books may be cumbersome on a working surface. Small-scale projects can be practised in which the pupil will need to use initiative and develop powers of organization. Both boys and girls will need training in skills and techniques which are essential to independent living despite a visual handicap.

5   From childhood to adolescence (social and personal development)

Influence of visual handicap on personal development

Unpredictability with inconsistent attitudes towards parents and teachers can be a well-known characteristic of adolescents as they attempt to adjust to change and search for identity, but idealistic and generous aspects of behaviour can be strongly evident at this stage of personal development too. Those who teach and counsel visually handicapped adolescents must be moved to consider whether lack of sight or defective sight is likely to be a source of additional stress and anxiety at this sensitive time.

Certainly it might be expected that doubts about personal acceptability and attractiveness and apprehension that the presence of visual handicap may limit career and marriage prospects would be experienced. Lowenfeld (1971) considers that the stages of adolescence through which the young person normally passes in growing up are likely to be encountered in the same sequence in the case of visually handicapped adolescents. However, the self-concept that he has developed by adolescence will be a crucial factor, governing the way in which such a young person tries to come to terms with new or newly perceived problems and opportunities in personal and working life.

A study of personality differences between blind and sighted children by Zahran (1965) reviews the literature which is divided between those who contend that blindness leads to compensatory behaviour which may be accompanied by introversion and even maladjustment, and those who find that the process of adjustment in blind persons is not significantly different from that of the sighted with regard to basic personality variables. Using matched groups of blind and sighted children tested with the Williams Intelligence Test for Children with Defective Vision, the researcher also constructed a Blind Children's Structured Interview, a Sentence Completion Test and a Semantic

Differential. He also used the Junior Maudsley Personality Inventory. The results of most of the tests showed a statistically non-significant difference in favour of the sighted, which, on balance, lends some support to the second point of view.

But Meighan (1971) on examining the self-concept of the visually handicapped adolescent reveals a fragility in this aspect of the personality in many of these young people evident to their teachers as either timidity or over-compensation. His study evidenced that on the Tenessee Self-Concept Scale the scores of the majority of the visually handicapped showed a distinctly negative direction with doubts about work achievement and implications of anxiety and unhappiness; identity scores were low revealing the tendency for these young people to see themselves as impoverished in terms of their physical self and in their behaviour although, perhaps remarkably, their levels of self-criticism approximated to the norm in the majority of cases.

A striking fact emerging from this study is that the scores of the visually handicapped had an almost universally recognizable pattern cutting across differences in sex and with little difference between demographic groups. The common factor of visual disability seemed to be the one that affected the scores profoundly to the extent of showing up profiles of striking similarity. The discussion which is a sequel to the enquiry, concludes than an attempt to resolve the tendency of fixing a negative identity should be considered as a major development hazard in the case of the visually handicapped adolescent. In view of the crucial role of the self-concept in all areas of striving this is indeed a vital matter of concern.

That lack of self-confidence about social competence, personal appearance and adjustment to blindness increases towards adolescence is shown in Miller's (1970) study in which Hardy's anxiety scale for the blind was used with 50 blind young people at a residential school, giving further point to the need these young people have for specialized training and an understanding of their needs in a social situation. The period of adolescence itself is late to begin such training; techniques and counselling to forearm the young person against the challenges and uncertainties that he will encounter as he faces adult life in a world designed primarily for those who see, should be introduced during his school years.

Self-concept in the years at school

The roots of his self-confidence or lack of it may well go deep into the feelings that the adolescent has had about his acceptance or rejection during his first school years. This in its turn can be dependent upon the relationship which he has been able to make with people whom he considers 'special', possibly reflecting in his own person the attitude of his parents towards his school and his teachers.

As he grows up his general confidence may be enhanced if he is able to develop basic skills at an age that is reasonably approximate to that of his seeing peers. Timely and effective training without over-stress can be helpful in enabling him to master day-to-day skills, such as those involving mealtimes, travelling and dressing and looking after himself in a way that will tend to minimize embarrassing situations which could otherwise be resented by the adolescent who is especially sensitive about the impression he makes on others. Indeed throughout his childhood and adolescence he may be vulnerable to the evident reaction of sighted people to his handicap.

The child who is obviously and evidently blind may have to bear with comments or even exclamations about this fact from seeing adults whom he encounters casually, whilst the child who is poorly sighted may have his difficulties ascribed to causes unrelated to his vision. It would hardly be surprising, therefore, for the visually handicapped adolescent to shrink from being noticed because of his handicap, although he is likely to be in a stronger position of tolerance if he has felt valued for himself and has experienced success; enthusiasm and interest in commonly accepted activities – swimming, stamp collecting, piano playing or singing can provide him with a talking point to share and a recognizable reason to increase his self-esteem.

In his primary school years the visually handicapped child will need both structured and unstructured situations in which to learn as much as possible about the people and the environment that surround him, through exploring, investigating and conversing; it must not be assumed that he will spontaneously be driven by curiosity to do so. Active play may need to be initiated, but through it he can be helped to externalize some of his inner conflicts. He needs the chance to destroy and build, to act out hate and love, and to test out his relationships with others. As he grows up his self-regard may risk being affected by the differences that he can become aware of between himself and his fully sighted friends and acquaintances, more especially if this is a subject of remark by onlookers. He may become aware that some things that they can do easily he cannot seem to do at all, such as recognizing distant objects or people, and there will be some things he can only do imperfectly or in an adapted way, such as playing football or reading. Resentment of these facts is possible but genuine success in its own right, such as the ability to read braille well or in having a good memory for the sports results can help him to be well regarded. His sense of security can be fostered by a stable framework of dependable events and reactions from adults, including steadiness and lack of dismay in the face of frustrations. These qualities he may need to draw on from his teacher upon whose reserves of emotional stability and tolerance he can depend.

Confidence is likely to have been helped if during his school years the visually defective pupil has had enough time to complete his tasks and secure his objectives, so that by the time he reaches adolescence, he has behind him repeated experiences of achievement; a childhood history littered with unfinished tasks and unachieved goals can undermine this.

When he progresses from primary to secondary school, the educationally blind or partially sighted child may, like his sighted peers, have a complete change of educational environment. This can be stimulating, and offer him the challenge of a larger community, bringing a fresh start that can flower into a greater maturity in social adjustment as a result of contact with older pupils. The opportunity for greater personal independence in a community should be afforded to him. In the case of some residential schools for the blind or the partially sighted a secondary school may take a large regional or even a national catchment of pupils, and thus be situated further from the pupil's home than his regional primary school with subsequently longer periods of separation from parents and family. Increasing attention is being given to providing opportunities to go home at week-ends from secondary schools in this category, and when distance makes this prohibitive, several long week-ends a term are usually organized. Some schools for blind and partially sighted children are described as 'all-age' and this means that the pupil can be in the same school from infancy to adolescence. Should this be the case it is important that situations are offered in which the pupil of secondary age has distinct reasons for feeling more adult and independent than in his primary years. He cannot make the transition from childhood to adolescence in one step, and needs the chance increasingly to make his own decisions, decide for himself what to eat, what to wear, what to do, what new pursuits to follow and what new responsibilities to undertake. One problem that can exist in an all-age school (and there are many for the blind) is that the early impressions that a child makes in his first years at school can cling to him and remain a talking point even after his growing personality has outstripped his initial reputation. It takes tolerance and understanding to give him the equivalent of a fresh start with the chance to take a step away from dependence on the adults who have often given him affectionate support in his early school years.

The visually handicapped adolescent who is over-dependent on adult approval may have had insufficient opportunities for independence, even at the level of making decisions about small matters, although his need to do this is increasingly well-understood in schools. Conversely inappropriate reactions of belligerence can be evident if he has had to struggle with adults for the chance to express his personality in his own way and to develop growing levels of personal autonomy. Either of these manifestations or an alternation of both can be expected as he tries to come to terms with himself as a young adult, perhaps with physical maturity at variance with emotional maturity. Cutsforth (1951) claims that there is a need for aggression and defiance in the blind youngster if he is to achieve and attain self-respect as the person he truly is, rather than conforming to the ideas of the sighted about what a blind young person should be like.

Development of communication and self-expression

It can be an asset for the young blind or partially sighted person if during his years of growing-up he has become meaningfully articulate; his inability to receive clearly, or perhaps at all, signals through non-verbal communication which the fully sighted would appreciate through glances, gestures and facial expressions, can make him seem insensitive to the appropriateness of the expression of his ideas and feelings in a particular context. He may give an impression of embarrassing shyness or brashly aggressive egocentricity that makes him particularly in need of the ability to distinguish, discriminate and formulate experience through language. Some difficulties in communication at least will be minimized if powers of verbal communication have been strengthened, developed and sharpened during his school years. Pride of place is frequently given in schools and colleges of further education for the visually handicapped to providing opportunities for self-expression through discussion of current affairs, through debates and in public speaking. This potentially valuable area can unfortunately all too easily become a time-filler consisting of desultory chat or undirected monologues by those who have developed the habit of indulging in this pastime.

Indeed talking at too great a length without pause for response can be a particular hazard for the young person whose blindness or severe visual limitation renders him unaware of warning signs of irritation or boredom from his listeners. Realizing the need for interaction in conversation demands a maturity and awareness that may not be easy to achieve.

Problems of this kind are referred to by Langford (1968) in describing his experience as a blind student at university. Some of the subtleties of inter-personal communication posed difficulties. For instance, when a sighted companion does not make the effort to speak, the blind student can pass by him in ignorant solitude, since in initiating conversation the onus is almost invariably on the sighted. This is a particularly awkward situation for those possessing a little sight, especially if they pretend to see more than is actually the case since normally sighted people expect to be recognized and greeted. Accumulated experience in inter-personal situations involving both the visually handicapped and the fully sighted before reaching adolescence is highly desirable in order to lessen the chances of embarrassment and inappropriate responses to situations.

Personal relationships and sex education

The basis of guidance and counselling for adolescents who are visually handicapped should, in essence, be comparable to that offered to young people generally, without an over-protective concern which could stunt their own developing powers of decision and responsibility. But in order to make responsible decisions these young blind and partially sighted people may need particular help, and may need to have information presented to them in a specialized way. This is certainly the case with regard to sex education, and it is essential that visually handicapped pupils should have full and appropriately presented facts as well as opportunities for discussion and questioning before they reach adolescence. Lest the provision of this area of education should be considered to usurp the role of the parent, who would ideally give such guidance, it is relevant to note that Langdon's Survey (1970b) sounded out the views both of parents and former pupils of schools for the blind. The majority of parents were firmly in favour of sex education being provided in school, whilst former pupils reported that although many of them had received what they considered to be adequate sex education by the time they reached the stage of further education, information could well have been given earlier and few had been alerted to the genetic aspects of their visual disabilities.

There are considerable difficulties to be faced and overcome in providing sex education for pupils who see poorly and especially for those who are totally and congenitally blind. The support and interest of the staff in the school as a whole with regard to education in matters relating to sex and family life is essential, since such a course will entail far more than simply a necessary provision of factual information as a classroom subject to pupils who are about 12 or 13 years of age.

The young blind or partially sighted child, like any other child, will need to have his questions about sex and reproduction, as about any other matter, answered in the language and at a level that he can understand. His questions are likely to show more ignorance of situations than if he could see, but the readiness with which he asks them is likely to depend for him, as for the sighted child, on the confidence and good relationship that exists between the child and the teacher. Through infant and primary stages of school increasingly detailed information can be presented to the pupil in this area of education within the framework of his increasing understanding. A child with enough vision to do so can be helped by illustrated books, but the child who is born blind will be in particular need of time spent in individual as well as in group discussion and explanation. The normal secondary school curriculum is likely to include biological facts, and films, whilst diagrams and models will be used. The time-honoured practice of keeping and looking after pets and their litters is of educative value here, too. But the child growing up must be helped to understand sexual impulses in himself. The presentation of factual information is not enough. Personal and social expectations, family, cultural and religious allegiances need sensitive and full consideration. Negative and prohibitive attitudes relating to sexual matters were sometimes encountered in schools for the blind in past years. An examination of day-to-day records and regulations can sometimes show a preoccupation with keeping boys and girls apart. The underlying fear may have been that the blind would marry the blind and in the relative absence of genetic counselling, an over-riding consideration seems to have been the apprehension that visual disabilities would be perpetuated or increased. Speculation as to whether such restriction made the visually handicapped youngsters of thirty years or more ago prone to guilt and ignorance must remain academic questions, but such rigidity seems unlikely to have contributed to their personal happiness. Today, most of the schools for the blind and the partially sighted are like most ordinary schools, co-educational, and visually handicapped youngsters who attend non-specialized schools will in the majority of cases be in a co-educational environment. Attempts to explore and find out about the human body including sexual experience will occur, whether they are permitted or not. But the young person, used to making his discoveries by touch, must understand that the tactile exploration of another person can be emotionally arousing. The responsibility of involving another person in an intense relationship needs to be understood. The presentation of graphic material and models as a means of imparting information will probably clarify the facts and processes only. Davis (1962) lays stress on the need for the communication of information about sex and family life to be accurate, adequate and with a content and expression at a level commensurate with the pupil's social maturity and his language level. He emphasizes that information and instruction about the physical aspects of sex-life and of the structure and function of the human body, must be related to the attitudes, expectations and values of the pupil's social milieu. As a matter of course, personal maturity and integrity are needed by teachers undertaking this aspect of education with the visually handicapped. Probably few of them would doubt that through the media and in discussion with each other the youngsters they teach are far from ignorant with regard to many of the facts about human sexuality, but this may be an added reason for ensuring that information is both full and well-understood. The presentation of facts, however, is quite different from understanding the facts in the context of human relationships. Co-educational settings in which the pupils are not discouraged from heterosexual friendships, and where boys and girls are brought up together as in a family may to some extent mitigate anxiety and curiosity about the opposite sex. In this matter the residential school environment presents a particular challenge to the adults who shape its ethos. A balance between encouraging individual freedom and responsibility to others is not easy to achieve, and the statement by Kahn (1965) that extreme permissiveness is the ultimate in authoritarianism can be especially true for the adolescent living in a community away from home.

Preparation for marriage and family life

Without statistical evidence on the incidence of marriage between boys and girls who are visually handicapped, one can only refer to impressions among staff of the schools in contact with their previous pupils and to past pupils re-visiting schools for reunions and social events. A superficial impression here would be likely to indicate that blind men are more likely than blind women to marry sighted partners, the situation with less severely visually disabled people being even less easy to define. There are, however, instances of totally blind housewives managing home and family chores with considerable efficiency and advising on kitchen layout and equipment to facilitate their housework.

That blind mothers can cope in a practical and systematic way with child rearing is illustrated by an article entitled 'Hints for Blind Mothers' (1970) giving specific advice on feeding, bathing and caring for the young child, walking with the toddler and generally meeting the needs of a young family. The question of whether young children suffer deprivation as a result of having severely visually handicapped parents is another area where enquiry would be of interest, but a study by Sheperdson (1967) emphasizes that since blindness is simply a characteristic in the life of a person and consequently of a family, it needs to be considered not as an isolated factor but as part of the total picture of the family's life. Sheperdson concludes, predictably, that mature blind parents with a secure, stable marriage, were seen to be capable of bringing up children who were well adjusted and secure. Interestingly, no significant difference in the effect on these children was noted if either one or both parents were blind, and whilst some deprivation was found in the case of a few children, this did not appear to be disabling in cases where the parents' blindness was the sole disability. Family problems and more severe degrees of deprivation seemed increasingly likely to occur when the parents' blindness was complicated by additional disabilities.

Reducing apprehensions about adult life

With so much emphasis on the media, and in advertisements, on the desirability of physical attractiveness, it would not be surprising to find some anxiety among visually handicapped adolescents with regard to lack of visual appeal and possible apprehension that marriage prospects or romantic attachments may be low for them. Much can be done to help visually handicapped adolescents in respect of appearance; the techniques of looking as good as possible are not very difficult to learn by the sighted, the partially sighted or the blind. Many sighted youngsters adopt the styles they find attractive from magazines, advertisements and from their friends and contemporaries. As with some other aspects of day-to-day living this is more of a 'learned' task for the blind or the very poorly sighted. At least three well-known cosmetic firms have worked out excellent schemes for the blind with regard to skin care and make-up and have demonstrators who will visit schools and colleges. This aspect of self-presentation should be as much fun as it is for the sighted girl, not over-emphasized but available. The appearance of the eyes or the face itself may be disfigured as a result of disease or accident and cosmetic operations or the provision of prosthesis can be particularly important to the adolescent. The response of sighted persons to physical appearance may be a factor to which the visually handicapped person is particularly sensitive. It can be all too easy for adults helping the blind and severely visually handicapped youngsters with the choice of clothes, to be over-influenced by the standards of attractiveness and acceptability of their own age groups. But mixing with sighted friends of a comparable age, shopping with them and establishing identity with them is vital for the young; an over-tidy, self-conscious blind adolescent may seem bizarre to his sighted colleagues, possibly resulting in lessening his chances of unremarked acceptance by them. In the more profound sense one cannot wholely educate for parenthood nor give training for falling in love, for these young people any more than for others. It is, nevertheless, possible to ensure that they are not ignorant and that the environment in which they grow up is neither over-protective nor, in the other extreme, irresponsible. The interest of parents and the guidance of teachers and care staff who have achieved their own measure of personal fulfilment in different life styles, can represent a range of mature ways of handling personal relationships that offer living reassurance to the adolescents who have more to come to terms with than many of their contemporaries.

6 The visually handicapped adolescent (further education, vocational guidance and placement)

Supportive and advisory services for the visually handicapped school leaver

The choice of a career that offers financial independence as well as giving inherent interest may be difficult for the visually handicapped adolescent and be a source of anxiety to him. He may reflect not only his own doubts and uncertainties with regard to the future, but also those of his parents. He may find himself with the same fears of being without a job as many other school-leavers, but with the additional burden of realizing that embarking on a particular career may be difficult because of his visual handicap.

However, there are for these young persons a number of supportive and advisory services available to help and specialized assessment and training centres offering a range of courses with a vocational aim. Greenhalgh (1974) gives a clear account of the services relating to the employment of people with restricted vision, listing the Department of Employment as responsible for the work of the Disabled Resettlement Officer and the Blind Persons Resettlement Officer, as well as the specialized assessment centres, training centres, sheltered workshops and home worker schemes. This department is also responsible for the provision of any aids and special equipment needed in employment, for the quota system in which a percentage of disabled persons must be included in the total work force, and for designated employment considered appropriate for handicapped employees. An educational responsibility overlaps the work of the Department of Employment in its responsibility for part of the youth employment services, and for the provision of careers advisers in schools.

The social services have a wide ranging function, notably in the provision of a social casework service and in the registration of handicap. These services may also give some vocational guidance, and specific advice on such matters as lighting and communication aids, tape-recorders and enlarged print books. In the case of the school-leaver, it is to be supposed that he will have already mastered typewriting and braille if he needs to use it, as well as mobility and orientation. He may, on the other hand, need to learn or improve these skills at a specialized assessment or vocational training centre, but he will be less likely to need help from the Social Services Department in these areas than the adventitiously blind adult.

Low vision aids are provided through the hospital service, and other aids and equipment are available through the Royal National Institute for the Blind. These include mobility aids, braille watches, braille and shorthand machines. The Institute is also responsible for vocational assessment and training centres, some specialized training provision, such as the School of Physiotherapy, and the commercial and telephony courses undertaken at Pembridge Place, London. The placement of prospective professional visually handicapped persons also comes under the aegis of the Institute. Although voluntary agencies on both local and national levels provide additional services complementing the statutory agencies, there is some overlapping in this provision, and some ambiguity because of the conflicting division between 'official blindness' and 'official partial sight'.

Development of personal independence and maturity

However wide-ranging the services, their effectiveness in helping the client depends greatly on the effectiveness of the client as a person. The young visually handicapped worker will need more than simply appropriate academic qualifications or specific aptitudes if he is to succeed in employment; marked personal immaturity or socially inappropriate behaviour, or the inability to manage daily living situations may partly negate other qualities and restrict or destroy opportunities that might otherwise have been promising.

This means that in its broadest sense career education begins when the pupil is young, and does not consist merely in terms of career information during the last years at school. The development of positive attitudes both personally towards the community and its resources is vital, together with increasing understanding of the nature of the jobs people do, and the way in which the life of the community is supported by the work contributions of people in many different spheres of occupation.

As vocational guidance becomes more specific the problem of unrealistic career ambition may have to be met. Lowenfeld (1971) captures this dilemma, when referring to the blind youth who experiences 'lure of the Car' and who is unable to come to terms with impossible wishes in regard to his future. Cunliffe (1970) finds that a patient approach can help to modify career choice without making the young person concerned feel frustrated or foolish. Initially, one has to consider what is meant by 'unsuitable' in a proposed career. The blind student who has graduated in medicine or become an artist is indeed an inspiration in terms of persistence, ability, and ingenuity in overcoming difficulties, but the realities of such exceptional achievements need to be explored carefully and sensitively. In this way, latent talent and ambition can so far as possible be directed into a course likely to culminate in a realistic career and personal fulfilment. Improbable career choices may be fed by parental hopes or by journalistic accounts of unusual successes which are biased towards the newsworthy. Increasing general maturity, the opportunity to undertake actual work experience and to discuss proposed courses of action with experienced staff and with class mates who have gained wider experience frequently means that the school-leaver will himself modify his career choice to one that is more realistically attainable. Unusual career ambitions should be taken seriously and the exact requirements in terms of training and qualifications carefully examined. Not only will this make it evident to the student that genuine and informed concern is being directed towards his enquiries, but in some cases such investigations may reveal areas of unexpected career opportunity for the visually handicapped. Demands for certain kinds of employment vary even from year to year, and there can be a risk of stereotyping employment with an over-close almost inevitable connection between certain handicaps and traditional occupations.

Preparation for employment and independent living

Cunliffe (1970) focuses attention on the gaps that can stretch between school life and its expectations, and the very different ones in the world of the factory or office; his words aptly describe the predicament of the young blind or severely visually handicapped youngster beginning work:

It is not generally realised to what extent handicapped youngsters require extra preparation for success in the work situation – as children they have been used to more special attention than they can receive in industry. In the strange industrial, even alien, atmosphere, they are scared, depressive and slow to learn – with shy adolescence they seek to piece together the shattered concept of the ideal adult and the dream future that has bolstered their living so far. What do they really know of charge-hands, foremen, managers, piece-rates, bonuses, unions, strikes, agitators, stoppages, undesirables, dogged tiredness, or even wage earning? These things are difficult to learn in a classroom from a pedagogue or in a crowd of children. This problem applies, of course, to all school leavers, but particularly, surely, to ours.

To what extent have the schools for the blind and for the partially sighted attempted to prepare their pupils for the realities of the working world and the challenges of independent life? Childs (1974) summarizes replies to questionnaires sent to nine schools for the partially sighted and seven schools for the blind in the UK. Careers guidance in the form of interviews with careers officers appeared to be emphasized during the last two years of school in the majority of instances and many examples of contact between careers officers and school-leavers are noted. Also general were attempts to prepare for job applications in interviews; the approach here was varied from mock interviews with adults to more general discussion of probable interview situations, sometimes in English lessons, sometimes in a separate scheme of lessons or lectures. Evidence was not given with regard to the effectiveness of this preparation in the real situation and feedback enabling the teacher to alter or modify this training would have been useful. The survey indicated that school visits to places of work were general and three of the partially sighted schools were quoted as having work experience schemes. Particularly good rapport had been established in one instance between the school and personnel staff in local factories where partially sighted pupils undertook one week of work in factory conditions each term. The importance of information indicating areas of success and of difficulty in the work situation are essential if such schemes are to be the result of a profitable use of time since the pupil will then not only have the benefit of work experience but will also have the opportunity of solving or at least mitigating some of the problems by discussing them with a teacher experienced in the needs of the visually handicapped.

Schemes of this kind can be helpful in easing the transition from the relatively short and well-ordered school day to the longer working day which may encompass hours of monotonous work on the one hand or, on the other, calls for initiative and independent thinking. In giving vocational assessment and guidance the dignifying nomenclature of 'careers advice' it must not be forgotten that for many young visually handicapped people the reality of their work situation will mean that they will spend many working hours in undertaking repetitive tasks, the type of work that they would undertake if they were not visually handicapped being perhaps a measure of the appropriateness of the work in which they actually engage.

Factors contributing to success in training programmes

The value of a positive philosophy in structuring training is emphasized by Kenmore (1975) who has the advantage of broadly based international experience in vocational assessment and placement programmes for the visually handicapped. In noting differences in career opportunities in a variety of situations she recognizes the existence of obvious restrictions in career choice and job opportunity resulting from visual limitations, but nevertheless emphasizes that these are heightened if poor education and poor social skills depress the levels of competence. Meanwhile she comments that successful programmes for the visually handicapped embody qualities of leadership, long-range planning, high standards of work, and attention to the differing needs of visually handicapped people. Factors which lessen opportunities for career choice and fulfilment are a lowered economy, increasing general unemployment and a lack of understanding by sighted persons of the ways in which visually handicapped people can succeed in work. Attention is drawn to the need for those planning career guidance and setting up vocational programmes to examine constantly and carefully the fields of work where there are scarcities of trained sighted workers, the marketing prospects for well-made products as well as the kinds of education, counselling and specialized training essential if the young visually handicapped person is to hold his own in the competitive world of work.

The two factors which, according to Venn (1964) are major considerations in successful work placement, are the effectiveness of the visually handicapped person himself as an individual and the extent to which those responsible for developing vocational programmes have kept up to date with scientific and technical developments.

School-leavers with partial sight

The adolescent leaving a partially sighted school and the partially sighted pupil from an ordinary school are in some ways in a less well defined position than those leaving schools for the blind who are likely to go to the specialized assessment centres or to the Royal National College for the Blind. Kell (1973) claims that the partially sighted school-leaver should be considered as a young person with potential and choice; his visual handicap being considered along with other factors such as his ability, disposition and ambition so that he receives maximum encouragement to aim at the highest level of work or training within his capability, rather than emphasizing his defective sight in terms of a primary limiting factor in further education or career placement. Her account of the attention given in schools for the partially sighted to career education indicates that most of these had a teacher with special responsibility for this crucial area even if it had to be combined with other teaching duties. Teachers in schools for the partially sighted contributing to this survey recommended that 'careers' should be regularly timetabled and carefully planned in a course beginning when the pupils were about 14 years old. They felt that the requirements of the less able partially sighted pupil were especially in need of attention. Visits to factories and offices should be undertaken with a constructive approach preceded by introductory information which could help to arouse active observation and should be followed up wherever possible by detailed discussion with representatives of the careers service. In addition, literature about job opportunities and training in the locality needs to be readily available. Whilst teachers of the partially sighted agreed that careers officers should be supplied with the medical, educational and biographical information relating to the young people they were attempting to place in employment, there was not general agreement about the advantage of registration of these young people as partially sighted persons.

The realities of the situation facing the partially sighted school-leaver are well understood by Wolffe (1975) who indicates that job requirements are rarely graded in terms of visual acuity. His work gives attention to the increasing emphasis on the functional level of vision, and he is mindful of the experience of those involved in the education of the partially sighted who have observed their pupils undertaking some highly complex or detailed tasks with unexpected success in terms of their visual acuity measurement. Predictive tests of employment capability are therefore being developed to provide information that is meaningful to those responsible for job placement. Whilst working on these Wolffe encountered problems requiring urgent solution. Although the provision of low vision acuity aids frequently results in marked improvement in performance in the use of residual vision, these aids, he found, were often not used and further studies investigating this omission from both a clinical and psychological point of view are needed. Attention to aids useful for distance vision in the form of contact lense telescopes is also felt to be important and further work on the possibility of variable focal spectacle lenses might increase the purposes for which low vision aids could be used in the work situation. But it is not only in the development of more flexible aids that problems arise. Wolffe is of the opinion that youngsters leaving a special school for the partially sighted have had too little experience of the sighted world of work to succeed in integrating into it and the careers and resettlement officers in their home districts, as well as their employers, might have little experience of the partially sighted and thus misunderstand the sources of some of their problems.

In some instances it is possible for the young partially sighted school-leaver to attend a course at an industrial rehabilitation unit. This can involve a team approach which includes particular attention to the needs of the partially sighted as shown at the

Birmingham Industrial Rehabilitation Unit; special aids are loaned from Exhall Grange School for the Partially Sighted and if these prove to be useful in the industrial situation they can subsequently be supplied when the trainee commences employment. Ferris (1975) describes the Unit's facilities as including training in welding, machine operating, woodwork, engineering, and outdoor activities such as gardening and brick-laying. Switchboard operating, secretarial work and draughtsmanship are available with facilities for using modern office equipment, and supervision as well as assessment is undertaken by specialized staff.

Some of the Department of Employment's industrial rehabilitation units provide school-leavers' work preparation courses which may be attached to local colleges of further education, whilst work orientation courses for handicapped school-leavers run by some authorities may include some partially sighted adolescents. Colleges of further education and training for the disabled, such as St Loye's at Exeter, will accept the partially sighted if they are considered suitable after assessment for the courses available. Kell (1973) in her survey of 285 partially sighted school-leavers from seven selected schools, observes that over a third of these young people left school to undertake some form of further education, and that the number of these young people able to find employment in unskilled factory work and as shop assistants appeared to be falling with the result that a much narrower range of occupation, particularly for girls, has been evident in recent years.

Interest in the particular needs of the partially sighted school-leaver is developing in colleges of further education, in some instances with reliance on the specialized help of the local education authority's advisers in visual handicap. An instance of such a development is evident in the North Nottinghamshire College of Further Education, whose Work Orientation Unit also provides courses geared to meet the needs of students who are mentally handicapped, partially hearing or deaf. These courses have an element of assessment as well as training and generally last for two years. They are within the broad spectrum areas of engineering, construction, business studies and management, general studies, fashion, hairdressing and retail trade. Work experience is undertaken with the aim of giving the students an opportunity to participate in open employment, sheltered employment, or work at home, according to their ability and circumstances. Hutchinson (North Nottinghamshire College of Education Orientation Prospectus, 1975) describes the benefit to students of work experience as largely consisting of increasing motivation towards employment and socialization by mixing with able-bodied people of all age groups. Close contact is kept both with the student and his temporary employer during the experience period, with subsequent feedback on problems and successes.

The severely handicapped school-leaver

Myers (1975) finds that even though much more needs to be done to provide suitable post-school situations in the case of those adolescents who are multiply handicapped or retarded, there are in some instances heartening indications of an improving situation for those leaving school; he exemplifies his optimism by giving case-histories of such people who have overcome considerable difficulties in order to win the opportunity to work, occasionally to earn a living, more frequently to benefit from social contacts and occupation away from their home or hostel.

There is obviously a need in the case of the severely multiply handicapped pupil with little or no sight to consider preparation for 'planned dependence' which, on first consideration, may appear to run counter to the efforts in helping the visually handicapped pupil to gain increased independence. However, the issues discussed by Gardner (1969) relating to the multiply handicapped school-leaver with some physical impairments, are highly relevant to the visually impaired adolescent who is also heavily multiply handicapped. In all such cases dependency if inevitable should be the result of planning and discussion and forethought, not an occurrence arising from default. It should also be continuously under review. The timely emphasis on social competence instead of over-emphasis on academic aims and the acceptance of a life-style that presents an alternative to independence is an essential and central feature of education for some visually handicapped adolescents with gross additional physical and intellectual impairments.

Specialized training in vocational and assessment centres and in further education

The schools for the blind and the partially sighted included in Child's (1974) survey appeared to be well-orientated in encouraging school leavers to go on to further education or to a period of vocational assessment. The two specialized vocational assessment centres at Hethersett near Reigate, and at Harborne in Birmingham and the Royal National College for the Blind have close links with schools for the blind and for the partially sighted. Originally these centres were strongly orientated towards the needs of the educationally blind with the emphasis on tactile methods of learning and training in such professions as audio-typing, braille shorthand, pianoforte tuning and repairs, and light engineering. It has been emphasized that the industrial situation may offer working conditions in which it is difficult to make the most effective use of fallible sight; for instance, when peering over moving machinery the situation can be dangerous. Consequently braille and tactile representation of diagrammatic work are used in the teaching at these centres. This may perhaps be for the first time for some of the adolescents with a little vision and resentment of it as an assumption of blindness can occur. Opinion remains divided with regard to the value as opposed to the heavy cognitive load of learning both braille and print reading whilst the pupil is still at school, but the ability to draw on either technique can certainly be of practical use to some adolescents with limited vision.

Both the specialized assessment and vocational training centres offer a curriculum of general education but with particular attention to the development of personal independence and the mastery of daily living skills. If this is considered in conjunction with the training already given in these areas in many schools for the visually handicapped it would appear that over the whole of school and further education a significant amount of time is spent on personal and domestic skills as well as on the mobility and travel techniques. Time spent early on perceptual training, hand-eye co-ordination, and training in the use of residual vision might well be expected to be effective in developing the underlying skills basic to a number of specific activities taught later in secondary school and in further education establishments. However, deterioration of vision, late onset of blindness, developmental retardation, absence from school, hospitalization and inappropriate early help or even lack of help can mean that by adolescence considerable time may need to be spent with some of the visually handicapped in quite specific training relating to day-to-day management of meals, travel, clothing, and shopping.

Educational programmes at the specialized centres for the visually handicapped provide an element of assessment as part of vocational guidance; much of this has a practical bias, for instance in the case of light engineering, in which course machine operating of various kinds can indicate the trainee's probable suitability for a more extended course in this work. Employment in light engineering can afford work well within the capabilities of some visually handicapped operators. Some adaptations to standard equipment, especially in those tasks in which speed and accuracy are important, can be made, for example, specialized jigs can be used for simple assembly jobs. Light crafts can give practice in manual dexterity. The claim is even made that hands and arms may be strengthened by such activities which can also show the worker's ability to follow instructions. Workshop practice usefully includes measuring and practical mathematics. Courses at the specialized assessment centres include the use of a number of braille instruments, including micrometers, since reliance on interpretation through touch can be necessary in some workshop situations.

Pre-telephony courses available at the specialized assessment centres not only give an indication of the suitability of a student for a longer telephony course, perhaps at Pembridge Place (RNIB College, London) but in any case practice in using this means of communication skilfully is of general value. Basic typing is likely to have been learned at school by many students but it has a role in the vocational assessment centres too. Again, the aptitude of a student can be assessed with the possible recommendation that a longer professional training in shorthand and audio-typing be considered. Competence in typing in its own right offers one of the most useful forms of communication between the blind or poorly sighted pupil and his fully sighted colleagues, teachers, and lecturers. Indeed it can sometimes be a surprise to discover the facility with which even a totally blind student can use an ordinary typewriter with the addition of a 'braille scale' fitted at the back to assist him in correct alignment and setting out of work. The term 'braille typewriter' is sometimes misapplied here. The function of the braille upward writer (e.g. Perkins Upward Writer) is to emboss braille symbols onto special manilla paper. Confusion can also exist in connection with the term 'braille shorthand' especially since the association of shorthand is normally with the graphic methods of Pitman or Gregg. However, a highly contracted form of braille referred to as 'Grade III' can be used on a particularly light portable upward writer, fitted with a spool to take a narrow ribbon of paper which receives the embossed codes. The paper strip can be slotted through a wooden guide for finger reading. This method enables some skilled and highly trained braille shorthand writers to achieve speeds of up to 180 words per minute and to undertake advanced examinations in shorthand and typewriting such as those set by the Royal Society of Arts. High speeds of work and a remarkable level of accuracy can also be obtained by some students appropriately trained in audio typing. The Royal National College for the Blind recognized by the Department of Education and Science since 1972 as a national college of further education for both blind and partially sighted has a long-established record of training and successful placement in commercial work of this nature, admitting students, either straight from school or after an initial period at one of the assessment centres. There are two interrelated aspects to the further education and training offered at this College. First, those aspects of personal competence including daily living skills which form a programme of budgeting, housekeeping, cookery, use of launderette and dry-cleaners, and travel techniques including long-cane mobility. Secondly, a general one-year course in further education which precedes more specialized vocational courses. This is of particular value to those students who need time to decide on appropriate further training or who have missed some aspects of their earlier education, perhaps through illness or deteriorating sight. The more advanced further education facilities prepare students with the appropriate ability for university places or for professional training elsewhere in physiotherapy, music or teaching. Even more specific and well-tried are the courses in commercial subjects leading to advanced qualifications in shorthand-typing and audio-typing described by Hayward (1975). The present courses for piano tuners and technicians are rooted in the traditional training developed early in the history of the College, but now ,incorporate not only pianoforte tuning and repairs but also accounts, business management, and typing, thus enabling the successful student to run his own business should he wish to do so. As a relatively remunerative career for students with initiative who enjoy travelling and meeting people this training has stood the test of time and offers particular attractions to those wishing to attempt to build up their own commercial enterprise. The London College of Furniture offers courses in piano tuning and repairs which have been undertaken by a small number of visually handicapped students.

Visually handicapped students in colleges and universities

The school-leaver may go straight on to an ordinary college of further education, to a polytechnic or to a university rather than to a college or assessment and vocational training centre specially geared to meet the needs of the visually handicapped. It is to be expected that there will be both advantages and drawbacks to this situation and the ability, adjustment, and confidence of these students will need to be considered on an individual basis together with the opportunities and limitations offered by the particular educational situations being considered. The limiting factors may result from encounters with members of staff who are not fully aware of the implications of visual handicap and who may consequently under-estimate difficulties in the work situation resulting from it, or conversely embarrass the student by patent over-concern. A teacher or lecturer experienced and trained in dealing with the visually handicapped can often quickly resolve problems relating to the learning situation and offer valid and well-tried solutions to them. In addition, it is improbable that there will be special opportunities for increasing the student's skill in mobility and personal independence. It is not enough to assume that placing such students in lodgings or a hall of residence at a distance from their college will provide them with a practical self-help course in mobility. It may be possible to enlist the help of the social services who can effectively give specific training here, but there is pressure for the services of appropriately qualified personnel and it must be ensured that help of this kind is given early in a student's course if it is required; without it the young visually handicapped person may be in a difficult situation in trying to balance between under- and over-dependence on sighted colleagues for day-to-day information, transport, and interpretation of material in lectures and classes that has been presented visually.

Set against these considerations there are nevertheless very real benefits for visually handicapped young people in many respects if they are well prepared and well supported in an ordinary tertiary educational situation. They are likely to have a wide choice of curriculum and probably most important of all, ordinary daily social interaction with sighted young people of their own age group compared with which the opportunities for 'mixing with the sighted' at a specialized centre may seem somewhat formal or contrived. The personal maturity and readiness of the individual to undertake further education in an ordinary situation, as well as the real, not simply the intended supportive services, need to be weighed carefully when decisions are made with regard to educational placement for these adolescents.

There are a number of quite specific techniques which can be adopted by the visually handicapped student who is working in an ordinary college or university setting. Many of these have been outlined in the report on study techniques compiled by the Open University (1974). The skill of the individual in all communication is stressed and also his need to develop the technique of intent listening with the ability to retain relevant and important data. It is rightly claimed that the tape-recorder skilfully used is an invaluable aid for the student who cannot or does not wish to rely on his sight for note-taking. Both cassette and reel-type recorders are useful, especially machines that have a built-in microphone whilst both an audible stop and an automatic stop are advantages. The development of the recorder with additional speed control giving the advantage of high-speed speech, is especially valuable for students, and may be considered as the nearest thing to visual scanning in reading. Earphones which eliminate background noise while recording also prevent disturbance to other students. Stress is laid upon the student's initiative in perfecting the method of recording that suits him best and is most appropriate to his studies as well as in noting ways in which others have succeeded, possibly making use of pre-recorded texts available from the

Royal National Institute for the Blind Students' Library. The Royal National Institute for the Blind offers a number of support services for visually handicapped students entering universities, polytechnics or colleges of education. These include payment for readers of sighted texts, grants for special equipment such as tape-recorders, and the services of an experienced counsellor and a careers officer who may be consulted while the student is undertaking a course in higher education or after its completion.

It is to be hoped that methodical habits of working will have been developed during school years by the visually handicapped student since much time can be wasted if notes and tapes are not labelled and stored in a systematic way for easy retrieval. Avis (1974) recommends the use of a filing cabinet to hold braille notes embossed on punched paper so that treasury tags with dymo-type labels can be used for easy recognition. In choosing sighted readers to help the blind student deal with his textbooks he considers that trained persons provide the most useful service. It can be particularly helpful for the blind student to have an embossed map of the campus of the college before he begins his studies and to have the chance to explore for himself the layout of lecture rooms and cloakrooms before the buildings become thronged with students. He is likely to gain self-respect as well as that of his fellow students if he does not have to depend upon them unduly for directions and assistance at the start of the course, and the initial impression that he makes may often have a lasting impact.

It may also be helpful to visit libraries at a quiet time if possible so that staff can give any additional help in tracking down reference books and journals. The student may have difficulty with notices displayed in corridors and dining rooms and it is important for him to establish as soon as possible the ways in which he will deal with such problems.

Progress in scientific, technological and social fields has increased the possibilities for the visually handicapped to participate in academic work and to engage in intellectual pursuits. Blindness in itself should in no way be connected with a deficiency of abilities, but an increasing effort should be made on an international basis to solve any training or technical problems that might limit either opportunity or prevent success. But the contribution of the blind student himself to this success may be heavily dependent upon his personality development as well as on his level of academic performance. Another factor likely to influence the successful conclusion of courses and to have a bearing on subsequent employment is the appropriate choice of subject at higher education level; studies of the humanities, economics, mathematics and music still hold primary place in the academic areas of training for blind students.

The need for co-operative effort in solving training and employment problems

An examination of current provision in the areas of vocational assessment and guidance, in further education and in specific job-training for the visually handicapped school-leaver poses the question as to how far the personal and career-orientated needs of these young people are being fully and realistically met under the present system of training which involves a unique example of co-operation between state departments, local authorities, and voluntary bodies.

However, a depressing problem can beset the school-leaver with a sight defect even if this is his only handicap. The possibility of lack of employment or of prolonged periods of waiting for employment or the opportunity to attend an occupational centre is, under present circumstances, inescapable. There is an understandable and frequently a well-founded optimism in the schools for these young people that they are being educated for an employed future. A teacher of the visually handicapped may well feel that the culmination of efforts in educating pupils is realized in their becoming financially and personally independent. However, it is also vital that tactics are worked out to combat the frustration, depression or, worst of all, procrastination that can develop if employment or occupation is not available. Interests can be followed, skills developed, and social contacts made and maintained even in the face of unemployment, but these possibilities must be discussed and considered frankly so that the visually handicapped adolescent has had some preparation for facing and coping with the situation of joblessness should it arise.

Visually handicapped people have attained success in a wide range of careers and professions. Venn (1964) considers that there are probably blind people in every profession one can think of, but that for the young graduate leaving university or tertiary education the vocational choices usually indicated are far more restricted and usually fall within the bounds of physiotherapy, school-teaching, university teaching, music, law, the church, and computer programming. Administration may be an avenue for those with first class honours degrees. In suggesting that new opportunities for careers should constantly be sought and examined Venn also emphasizes that the essence of placement combines the right person with the right job. In order to achieve this there is a need for individualized instruction and planning with and for each young person by staff cognisant of the problems and potential of each blind and partially sighted young person under their tuition and guidance.

The varied ways in which the visually handicapped school-leaver may reach employment present what appears to be a fragmented picture. There is considerable and increasing awareness of the demands of the world of work in the special schools for the blind and the partially sighted; there is a high level of expertise and co-ordination of services in the specialized vocational assessment centres and the Royal National College for the Blind, and there are continuing examples of young people engaging and succeeding in courses in ordinary colleges and universities. In theory there seems to be an exciting opportunity for those who have both the experience and knowledge of the needs of the visually handicapped in work and further education and those who can offer the richness of a broad curriculum and wide-ranging education opportunities to be able to co-operate in reducing this fragmentation. However, it is not always sufficiently realized that a quick visit to an established centre for the visually handicapped or a telephone call or letter requesting information on the provision of specialized equipment or the adaptation of material may be a minimum and somewhat insufficient answer to the problems that a young visually handicapped person may encounter in an environment designed for the fully sighted. Careful preparation at the time of the student's acceptance to courses and training through discussion with those providing it and with a teacher or lecturer who is both trained and experienced not only in the techniques helpful to the visually handicapped but also in the particular requirements of this age-group, would seem to be a more thorough approach. It is to be hoped that there will be increasing recognition that different forms of training and tertiary education are needed in the very different requirements of visually handicapped adolescents. Those already offering excellent and well-tried schemes have much to contribute, but information and experience are needed to increase the opportunities for visually handicapped students to enjoy education and training alongside their sighted colleagues. At the same time they must receive the expert help and support that they deserve.

7 Assessment of the intellectual, social and educational attainments of visually handicapped children

Background information useful in the assessment of visually handicapped children

The assessment of the intellectual levels, the social adjustment and the educational attainment of visually handicapped children can be a time-consuming procedure often requiring the administration of an appropriate test on an individual basis and pre-supposing a knowledge of the ways in which sight deficiency or loss may have affected not only the present but also the past experience of the child. Some understanding of the response patterns of blind children is necessary, for example, in their use of braille for communication, if a true understanding of their life style is to be achieved. Psychologists may see few visually handicapped children, especially those who are totally blind, and yet even with all the attendant difficulties the value of objective evaluation is unquestionable. The purpose for which assessment is being undertaken, however, must be clearly borne in mind; possibly it may be required in connection with recommendations for forthcoming educational placement, or as a measure of the suitability of existing placement, or perhaps as a gauge of any apparent disparity between the pupil's potential and his performance in school. Sometimes, those engaged in psychological and educational research need a series of measurements, amongst which an intelligence quotient is requisite, but the relatively low numbers of visually handicapped children in the UK necessitates discretion with regard to such requests in order that over-testing of the children does not ensue.

In order to undertake the level of assessment that can lead to useful guidance and contribute to wise decisions about school placement or remedial programmes it is essential that the psychologist or teacher is in possession of current information with regard to the child's degree of sight. He should also have a history which shows data on the age of onset of visual loss or its deterioration since the possession or lack of visual memories can affect some concepts. The child's previous educational experience, his exposure to pre-school counselling, together with records of protracted illness or periods in hospital, will also help to give essential background information. Parental attitudes towards the child and his handicap, his relationship with peers and siblings, will also be relevant in attempting to obtain a rounded picture of the child.

Tests for the normally sighted that have been used with visually handicapped subjects

Tobin (1977) has compiled what he describes as a brief introductory listing, with references, of tests for the normally sighted that have been used with visually handicapped subjects. The list is quite an extensive one suggesting among others tests in the area of language development:

The Illinois Test of Psycholinguistic Abilities (ITPA)
The Peabody Picture Vocabulary Test
The Modern Language Aptitude Test (Psychological Corporation, New York).

Tests tapping a wider area of aptitudes include:

California Psychological Inventory (CPI)
Cattell Infant Intelligence Scale
Columbia Mental Maturity Scale

Suggestions for assessing areas involving sensory or perceptual capacities include:

Wepman Auditory Discrimination Test
Visual Efficiency Scale (Barraga)

Aspects of personality may be measured by:

Junior Maudsley Personality Inventory
Bell Adjustment Inventory
California Psychological Inventory
Minnesota Multiphasic Personality Inventory (MMPI)

Further tests are suggested in connection with performance areas, for example:

The Purdue Pegboard
Sequin Formboard
Bennett Hand-Tool Dexterity Test
Cranford Small Pts Dexterity Tests

A full and informative description of testing procedures currently in use for visually handicapped children in the USA is given by Bauman (1972). Her list includes the Haptic Intelligence Test (Shurrager), the Stanford Kohs Block Design Test, and the Roughness Discrimination Test – considered useful as an aid in predicting ability to discriminate braille symbols.

Tests used in schools for blind and partially sighted children

In the UK a group of head teachers and class teachers from schools for the blind and the partially sighted, under the Chairmanship of M. B. M. Lumgair, gave attention to problems in the assessment of the visually handicapped child's progress, and the continuous day-to-day assessment of his educational attainments. They also considered effective ways of reporting the information obtained to parents and others concerned with the child's progress. The recommendations from this group of widely experienced practitioners included not only a recognition for the need of objective measurement of a child's intellectual functioning and his educational attainment but also diagnostic evaluation of his learning difficulties and a measure of his social–emotional adjustment.

Many of the tests suggested by this group were recognized as being standardized for use with sighted children. This was especially the case in areas of attainment, except for the specialized F. H. G. Tooze (1962) and Lorimer (1962) tests designed to assess the speed and accuracy of braille reading. The batteries of tests suggested as useful were as follows:

Early infancy

Gessell Developmental Schedules	Houber, New York
Griffiths Mental Developmental Scale	University of London Press

2 +

Merrill Palmer Performance Scale	
Wechsler Pre-school and Primary Scale of Intelligence (WPPSI)	Psychological Corporation, New York

Revised Stanford Binet Form L/M	Harrap

5 +

Wechsler Intelligence Scale for Children (WISC)	Psychological Corporation, New York
Raven's Coloured Matrices	Lewis.
Williams Intelligence Test for Children with Defective Vision	National Foundation for Educational Research, Slough

In areas of attainment the following were considered of some if not universal use for visually handicapped pupils:

Graded Word Reading Test,	P. E. Vernon, University of London Press
Graded Word Reading Test,	C. Burt, University of London Press
Diagnostic and Attainment Testings,	F. Schonell and F. Eleanor, Oliver & Boyd
Holborn Reading Scale,	A. Watt, Harrap
Standard Reading Tests,	J. C. Daniels, and H. Diack, Chatto & Windus
Analysis of Reading Ability,	Marie Neale, Macmillan
Bristol Achievement Tests (Maths) (English Language) (8 +),	Brimer, Nelson
GAP Reading Comprehension Test,	J. McCleod, Heinemann

Specialized tests for braille learners

Braille Speed Test,	F. H. G. Tooze, College of Teachers of the Blind
Braille Recognition Test,	J. Lorimer, College of Teachers of the Blind

Perception

Bender Visual Motor Gestalt test
Frostig Developmental Test of Visual Perception (4 +)
Illinois Test of Psycholinguistic Abilities (ITPA)
Reynell Developmental Language Scales

ASSESSMENT OF EDUCATIONAL ATTAINMENTS

Interests and emotional stability

APU Occupational Interests Guide,	J. Closs, University of London Press
Junior Eysenck Personality Inventory,	S. Eysenck, University of London Press
Manchester Scale of Social Adaptation,	E. Lunzer, NFER Slough
Children's Behaviour Questionnaire,	M. Rutter, Journal of Clinical Psychology
Bristol Social Adjustment Guide,	D. M. Stott, University of London Press
A Social Maturity Scale for Pre-School Blind Children,	Maxfield and Bucholz, American Foundation for the Blind
Vineland Social Maturity Scale,	NFER, Slough

Since the Williams Test and the Maxfield Bucholtz Adaptation of the Vineland Social Maturity Test are the only measures with normative data relating to the visually handicapped, results from the other tests suggested would need to be interpreted with caution.

There are some problems in using standardized tests for sighted children with visually handicapped subjects. The child who needs to use braille may be handicapped in the mechanics of reading or marking test material or the context may present him with problems that are inappropriate to his experience. The infinite gradations in potential difficulty resulting from various degrees and types of defective sight in the visually handicapped pose considerable problems for the tester. Both in the USA and the UK the Wechsler Intelligence Scales are considered useful measures across the full range of visually handicapped as well as sighted subjects. Where changes in timing or method of presentation of test material are necessitated, such alterations may influence the meaning of the scores obtained.

Tests standardized on visually handicapped subjects

There are obvious advantages in using tests designed for and standardized on a cohort of visually handicapped children. The most extensively used measurement of intelligence quotient for

147

blind and partially sighted pupils in the UK is the Williams Test for Children with Defective Vision.

The author of this was particularly aware of the difficulties inherent in the use of print material as some subjects with defective sight might find this a slow, difficult, or even an impossible medium to use. To substitute braille for print, may, however, merely create different problems since the subject may have poorly developed tactual discrimination, or an insufficient knowledge of the braille code. Difficulties in adapting symbolic material for use in the testing situation still, to a great extent, await solution, with the result that in a test such as that designed by Williams, there is heavy reliance on verbal confidence. Early work on the mental testing of blind children was undertaken by Hayes, particularly in his revision of the Stanford Revision of the Binet Simon Tests. His 1923 guide to the intelligence testing of the blind has been referred to as 'the scissors and paste test' since substitute items considered more appropriate than the original were pasted over those in the Binet Simon suited only to the sighted. Hindsight enables one to be critical of this approach, but it was indeed the beginning of the serious consideration of difficulties in the psychological assessment of blind children.

Subsequently, work in Great Britain was being developed by Langan who evolved a scale based on the Terman Merrill and Stanford Binet individual tests. Discarding those parts of the test inappropriate to the blind, she selected all the verbal items Forms L and M. Published in 1945, as an adaptation of the Binet this test was tried out extensively on visually handicapped children in 1948. In using this test Williams noted the extent to which children with some vision scored highly on performance items compared with the low scores in these areas gained by the totally blind, although some of the latter evidenced good levels of intelligence. This conclusion led her to construct, in 1956, a single test scale for blind and partially sighted children; this test is predominantly verbal but with a few unscored performance items to lend variety of activity to younger children and to offer the opportunity of observing their manipulation of objects. The test is administered on an individual basis, to subjects in a 5 to 15 age span who are described as either blind or with insufficient sight to read printed tests for the fully sighted with ease; it was standardized on a population of children whose vision measured on the Snellen Chart was less than 6/60. This test is widely used in the UK for children whose sight is within these limits and it should discriminate in the 8 to 13 year age-group between the very retarded and the very bright (that is with intelligence quotients measured on the Scale from 50 to 150) whilst with subjects in the younger age range from 5 to 8 years it should discriminate from the dull to the very bright (Williams notes a commencing score of 80 to 85 on the Scale) referring to probable retardation if a score below 80 is measured for subjects in this age-group. When used with the 13 to 15 age-group it should discriminate from the retarded to the bright (50 to 120). Williams was the first to concede that the quotient obtainable from her test was a blanket term, within which children with comparable scores might possess different kinds of ability. The final version of the test contains graded items which include recognition of verbal absurdities, comprehension, including that of abstract terms, sentence memory and verbal reasoning. Short-term memory items include repetition of forward and reversed digits. Problem solving involving ingenuity and making inferences also tested verbal memory since the questions were posed and the answers attempted orally. The unscored performance items included the sorting and matching of small objects, bead threading to a given pattern and the recognition of mutilated objects. Indeed, since the development of this test the whole concept of the use of the intelligence quotient has been subject to question but objective measurements that show reliability and validity have not been devised to supersede it. The standardized procedures for administering the test must be observed and responses scored according to the criteria given. This necessitates familiarity with the test on the part of the examiner who should be free to behave in an easy natural manner as well as being able to observe the subject's reactions to the questions he is asked. Conversation between the tester and subject is permissible and directions may be repeated but not explained. This makes the administration of the test a somewhat lengthy procedure, but over the years, since it was originally developed, it has continued to be used extensively in schools for the blind and the partially sighted to yield objective information to teachers and those engaged in research relating to the visually handicapped.

Assessment of social maturity in blind children

The other specialized test for visually handicapped children widely used both in the USA and the UK has a different purpose and a different age catchment. This is the adaptation from the Vineland Social Maturity Scale published after extensive trials and refinements in 1957 as the Maxfield Bucholz Scale. Since the subjects in this case are the pre-school visually handicapped it is necessary to elicit the required information of their typical behaviour by means of interview with the child's parent, teacher or house-mother. The items in the earliest stages of this assessment are predictably concerned with physical actions as basic as the ability to balance the head, and later to pull the body up unaided into a standing position. Further items measure social competence in areas of self-help such as dressing and levels of social adjustment in play and in group situations. The upper age limit for using this test is six years old, thus it is a useful indicator of levels of social competence in the child beginning school.

Longitudinal study of visually handicapped children

Tobin has used a Piagetian approach to yield interesting objective data on the pattern and sequence of cognitive development in visually handicapped children. His study on *Conservation of Substance in the Blind and Partially Sighted* (1972c) indicates a marked lag in this area, particularly in the case of blind subjects although a few of these were able to match levels normally attained by fully sighted children of the same age. Simple tests of this nature are not difficult to administer and can undoubtedly show the levels of concepts attained by individual children. The interpretation of the results, however, particularly outside the control of a disciplined and carefully structured experimental framework such as Tobin's Longitudinal Study (commenced 1971) require both skill and an insight into the implications of visual handicap.

Clearly there is scope for the future development and scrupulous standardization of test material useful for the psychological assessment of visually handicapped children, and just as clearly the problems of constructing such material with insight and validity are great.

Bibliography

ARGLES, E. (1971), 'The Mary Sheridan Unit', *Teacher of the Blind*, 60(1), pp. 8–11.

AVIS, M. (1974), 'Study Methods for the Visually Handicapped', Conference Report, Open University, Milton Keynes, pp. 9–10.

BARRAGA, N. C. (1964), *Increased Visual Behavior in Low Vision Children*, Research Series no. 13, American Foundation for the Blind, New York.

BARRAGA, N. C. (1970), *Teacher's Guide for Development of Visual Learning Abilities and Utilization of Low Vision*, American Printing House for the Blind, Louisville, pp. 1–6.

BARRAGA, N. C. (1974), *The Visually Handicapped Child in School* (ed. Lowenfeld), Constable, pp. 126–36, 143–6.

BARRAGA, N. C. (1976), *Visual Handicaps and Learning*, University of Texas at Austin, Wadsworth, California, pp. 12–16.

BAUMAN, M. K. (1972), *The Visually Handicapped Child* (ed. Lowenfeld), Constable, chapter 4, pp. 93–111.

BENTON, A. L. (1963), *The Revised Visual Retention Test*, Psychological Corporation, New York.

BIRCH, *et al.* (1966), *School Achievement and the Effect of Type Size on Reading in Visually Handicapped Children*, Co-operative Research Projects, University of Pittsburgh, no. 1766.

BISHOP, V. (1971), *Teaching the Visually Limited Child*, Thomas, Springfield, pp. 36–40.

BONHAM, M. H. (1967), 'The Workshop in Action', Fourth Quinquennial Conference, International Council of Educators of Blind Youth, Watertown, Mass., pp. 258–60.

BONHAM, M. H. (1975), 'The Braille Reading Scheme', *Teacher of the Blind*, 63(2), pp. 32–6.

BURROUGHS, G. E. R. (1957), *A Study of the Vocabulary of Young Children*, Oliver & Boyd, Edinburgh.

CARROLL, H. M. C. AND HIBBERT, F G. (1973), *Perceptual Ability in a Class of Partially Sighted Children*, Schindele Verlag no. 3, Karlsruhe, pp. 106–18.

CENTRAL ADVISORY COUNCIL FOR EDUCATION (1967), *Children and their Primary Schools* (Plowden Report), HMSO.

CHAPMAN, E. K. (1970), *Home Economics* (24 articles), College of Teachers of the Blind, pp. 87–9.

CHAPMAN, E. K. AND WILSON, S. (1970), *Books and Blind Children* (24 articles),

College of Teachers of the Blind, pp. 45–7.

CHILDS, J. (1974), 'Training for independence and leisure', *Teacher of the Blind*, 62(4), pp. 116–28.

CLARE, SISTER (1965), 'Experiment in integration', *Teacher of the Blind*, 53(2), pp. 72–4.

CLARKE, E. (1967), 'The needs of young blind children and their parents', *Teacher of the Blind*, 56(1), pp. 18–24.

COLLEGE OF TEACHERS OF THE BLIND (1956), *Handbook for School Teachers of the Blind*, pp. 87–101.

COLLEGE OF TEACHERS OF THE BLIND (1974), *The Family Books*, Handbook to the Reading Scheme.

CRATTY, B. T. AND SAMS, T. A. (1968), *The Body Image of Blind Children*, American Foundation for the Blind, New York, pp. 41–3.

CUNLIFFE, W. (1970), 'A treatment of unrealistic choice in vocational guidance', *Teacher of the Blind*, 58(3), pp. 65–9.

CUTSFORTH, T. D. (1951), *The Blind in School and Society*, American Foundation for the Blind, New York.

DAVIDOW, M. E. (1966), *The Abacus Made Easy*, Overbrook School for the Blind.

DAVIDSON, I. F. W. K. (1975), *Handbook*, Ontario Institute for Studies in Education.

DAVIS, J. C. (1962), 'The assessment of intelligence of visually handicapped children', *International Journal for the Education of the Blind*, 12(2) pp. 48–51.

DEARDEN, K. F. (1969), 'Theory and practice in education', *Listener*, June, pp. 851–3.

DEPARTMENT OF EDUCATION AND SCIENCE (1972), *The Education of the Visually Handicapped* (Vernon Report), HMSO, pp. 32–3, 131–7, Appendix F.

DOLCH, E. W. (1927), *Journal of Educational Research*, Illinois, no. 16, pp. 16–27.

DOUGLAS, J. W. B., ROSS, J. M. AND SIMPSON, H. K. (1968), *All our Future*, Peter Davis.

DUGMORE, E. (1973), 'Mobility exercises with the partially sighted', National Association for the Education of the Partially Sighted, *Journal*, October, pp. 6–8.

EAMES, T. H. (1937), 'A frequency study of physical handicaps in reading disability and unselected groups', *Journal of Educational Research*, no. 29, pp. 1–5.

FERRIS, F. (1975), 'New rehabilitation unit gives hope for employment', *Eyepiece*, 1(4), pp. 4–6.

FINE, S. R. (1968), 'Blind and partially sighted children', *Education Survey*, no. 4, HMSO, pp. 11–13, 15–20.

FINE, S. R. (1975), 'Registration and notification', *Child Care, Health and Development*, 5(1), pp. 309–13.

FLETCHER, R. C. (1968), 'Educating the blind adolescent', *New Beacon*, 7(618), pp. 254–8.

FRAIBERG, S., SMITH, M. AND ADELSON, E. (1969), 'An educational programme for blind infants', *Journal of Special Education*, 3, pp. 121–39

FRANCIS-WILLIAMS, J. (1966), 'Special educational problems of children with minimal cerebral dysfunction', *Teacher of the Blind*, 54(2), pp. 31–6.

GARDNER, L. (1969), 'Planning for planned dependence', *Special Education*, 58(1), pp. 27–30.

GETLIFFE, E. H. (1962), *Proceedings of the International Conference of Education of Blind Youth (Hanover)*, Perkins School for the Blind, Watertown, Mass., pp. 7–13.

GETTEGNO, C. (1962), *Words in Colour*, Educational Explorers.

GIBSON, E. J. (1953), 'Improvement in Perceptual Judgments as a Function of Controlled Practice or Training', *Psychological Bulletin*, 50, pp. 401–43.

GOMULICKI, B. R. (1961), *The Development of Perception and Learning in Blind Children*, Psychological Laboratory, University of Cambridge, pp. 52–8.

GREENBERG, L. (1969), 'Map Designs for Partially Sighted Students, An Investigation into White Versus Black Line Symbology', PhD thesis, University of Washington, pp. 1–160.

GREENHALGH, R. (1974), 'Services, related to employment for people with restricted vision, *Oculus*, January, pp. 6–7.

GREENWOOD, E. (1975), 'The Braille Reading Scheme', *Teacher of the Blind*, 62(2), pp. 32–5.

GRUNWELL, I. (1974), 'Vocational guidance', *Eyepiece*, 1(2) pp. 10–12.

GUTKIND, E. A. (1952), 'Race relations without conflict', *Social Work*, London, 9(3) pp. 707–8.

HARCOURT, B. (1975), *Child Care, Health and Development*, 5(1), pp. 315–24.

HAYES, M. (1941), *Contributions to a Psychology of Blindness*, American Foundation for the Blind, New York.

HAYES, S. P. (1923), 'The new revision of the Binet tests for the blind', *New Outlook for the Blind*, 17(3), pp. 26–8.

HAYWARD, B. (1975), 'The Royal Normal College', *Eyepiece*, I(5), pp. 10–11.

HEBB, D. A. (1937), 'The innate organization of visual activity: perception of figures by rats reared in total darkness', *Journal of Genetic Psychology*, 52, pp. 101–26.

HECHLE, B. (1974), *The Family Books* (Handbook to the Reading Scheme), College of Teachers of the Blind.

HECHLE, B. (1975), 'Teaching Children to Write in Braille', *Teacher of the Blind*, 64(1) pp. 6–9.

HEDLEY, E. A. (1972), *Overcoming Handicap*, Mills & Boon, pp. 53–62.

HENDERSON, P. (1974), *Disability in Childhood and Youth*, Oxford University Press, pp. 28–39.

HESLINGA, K. AND VAN 'T HOOF (1968), 'Sex education of blind-born children', *New Outlook for the Blind*, 62(1), pp. 15–21.

HILDRETH, H. K. (1947), 'The effect of visual training on existing myopia', *American Journal of Ophthalmology*, 30, pp. 1573–6.

HILLS, J. (1974), 'Teach-in for Parents (Hampshire)', *Teacher of the Blind*, 63(1), pp. 16–21.

'HINTS FOR BLIND MOTHERS' (1970), *New Beacon* (anon.), 54(635), pp. 58–63.

JAMES, G. A. AND CAMPBELL, D. (1975), 'A practical course in map-making', *Teacher of the Blind*, 64(1), pp. 4–6.

JASTRZEMBSKA, Z. S. (1976), *The Effect of Blindness and Other Impairments on Early Development*, American Foundation for the Blind, New York, pp. 11–13.

JOHN AIRD SCHOOL (1975), Information Sheet no. 1, *Teacher of the Blind*, 64(2), pp. 58–61.

JOINT COUNCIL FOR THE EDUCATION OF HANDICAPPED CHILDREN (1975), *Integration or Segregation?*

KAHN, J. H. (1965), *Human Growth and the Development of Personality*, Pergamon Press, Oxford, pp. 182–4.

KAPLAN, A. I. (1966), 'Development of residual vision functions in profound impairment of the visual analyzer', *Mental Development and Sensory Defects*, 18th International Congress of Psychology, Moscow, pp. 261–5.

KATZ, A. H. (1961), *Parents of the Handicapped*, Thomas, Springfield, pp. 126–36.

KELL, J. (1973), *Stresses in Children* (ed. Varma), University of London Press, pp. 116–26.

KENMORE, J. R. (1960), 'How a public school programme can meet the developmental needs of blind children', *Exceptional Children*, December, pp. 212–15.

KENMORE, J. R. (1975), 'International survey of training and employment opportunities for the visually handicapped', *The Educator*, 3(1), pp. 3–4.

KENYON, E. L. (1967), 'Diagnostic Appraisal at the Boston Centre for Blind Children', *Proceedings of the Fourth Quinquennial Conference*, International Council of Educators of Blind Youth, Watertown, Mass., pp. 70–9.

KOOYMAN, W. J. J. (1967), 'Physical education of pupils with defective vision and problems of orientation', *Teacher of the Blind*, 58(4), pp. 99–105.

LAIRY, G. C. AND HARRISON-NOVELLO, A. (1973), 'The Blind Child and its Parents', American Foundation for the Blind, *Research Bulletin*, no. 25, pp. 1–25.

LANGDON, J. N. (1968), 'A matter of concern', *New Beacon*, 52(612), pp. 282–6.

LANGDON, J. N. (1969), 'Some cause for satisfaction', *New Beacon*, 53(622), pp. 112–3.

LANGDON, J. N. (1970a), 'Parents talking', *New Beacon*, 54(643), pp. 282–8.

LANGDON, J. N. (1970b), 'Sex education – a survey of opinion', *Teacher of the Blind*, 59(1), pp. 30–5.

LANGFORD, J. (1968), 'Going to university', *New Beacon*, 52(618), pp. 258–60.

LANSDOWN, R. (1969), 'What the researcher doesn't know', *Special Education*, 58(4), pp. 20–5.

LANSDOWN, R. (1975), 'Partial sight – partial achievement', Southern and Western Regional Association for the Blind, *Regional Review*, no. 60, pp. 3–6.

LEONARD, A. J. (1966), 'Experimental maps for blind travel', *New Beacon*, 50(7), pp. 32–5.

LEONARD, A. J. (1967), 'Mobility as a school subject', *Teacher of the Blind*, 55(4), pp. 102–4.

LIGHTFOOT, W. (1948), *The Partially Sighted School*, Chatto & Windus, pp. 10–12.

LORIMER, J. (1962), *The Lorimer Braille Recognition Test*, College of Teachers of the Blind.

LORIMER, J. (1975), 'The measurement of Braille reading skills in blind children', Southern Regional Association for the Blind, *Report* no. 66, pp. 12–19.

LOVATT, M. (1970), 'Mathematics and Slow Learners', *Special Education*, 59(3), pp. 15–70.

LOWENFELD, B. (1959), 'The Blind Adolescent in a Sighted World', *Exceptional Children*, 25, pp. 310–15.

LOWENFELD, B. (1969), *Blind Children Learn to Read*, Thomas, Springfield.

LOWENFELD, B. (1971), *Our Blind Children* (3rd ed), Thomas, Springfield.

LUMGAIR, M. B. M. (1974), 'The Assessment and Recording of Progress', unpublished report, Edinburgh.

LYNDON, W. T. AND MCGRAW, M. L. (1975), *Concept Development for Visually Handicapped Children*, American Foundation for the Blind, New York, pp. 11–28.

MARSHALL, G. (1969a), 'Detecting visual dysfunction', *Special Education*, (111), pp. 21–3.

MARSHALL, G. (1969b), 'The Pre-school Child with a Visual Handicap', *Eyepiece*, 1(2), pp. 16–23.

MAXFELD, K. E. (1936), 'The spoken language of the blind pre-school child: a study of method', *Archives of Psychology*, 201.

MEIGHAN, T. (1971), *An Investigation of the Self-concept of Blind and Visually Handicapped Adolescents*, American Foundation for the Blind.

MILLER, W. H. (1970), 'Manifest Anxiety in Visually Impaired Adolescents', *Educating the Visually Handicapped*, 2(3), pp. 91–5.

MOMMERS, M. J. C. (1975), 'The Louis Braille British Conference on Research into Reading and Listening by the Visually Handicapped', Southern Regional Association for the Blind, *Report* no. 66, pp. 27–42.

MURRAY, W. (1964), *Ladybird Key Words Reading Scheme*, Wills & Hepworth.

MYERS, S. O. (1975), *Where Are They Now?*, Royal National Institute for the Blind.

NATIONAL FEDERATION OF THE BLIND AND ASSOCIATION OF BLIND AND PARTIALLY SIGHTED TEACHERS AND STUDENTS (1973), *Education for the Visually Handicapped*.

NEALE, M. D. (1958), *Analysis of Reading Ability*, Macmillan.

NORRIS, M., SPAULDING, P. J. AND BRODIE, F. H. (1957), *Blindness in Children*, University of Chicago Press, pp. 5–10.

OPEN UNIVERSITY (1974), *Study Methods of the Visually Hamdicapped*, Report on Birmingham Course, pp. 9–10.

PARK, G. E. AND BURRI, C. (1943), 'The effects of eye abnormalities on reading difficulty', *Journal of Educational Psychology*, no. 34, pp. 420–30.

PARMELEE, A. M. (1966), 'Developmental Studies of Blind Children', *New Outlook for the Blind*, pp. 177–9.

PARTIALLY SIGHTED SCHOOL LEAVER, WORKING PARTY REPORT (1974), *Teacher of the Blind*, 63(1), pp. 9–16.

PECK, O. S. (1925), 'Chronological retardation and promotion needs of pupils in sight saving classes', *Sight Saving Class Exchange*.

PICKLES, W. J. (1966), 'Surface Representation and the Blind', *New Beacon*, 50(589), pp. 123–5.

PICKLES, W. J. (1970), *Teaching Maths and Science to the Blind*, RNIB.

PITTAM, V. G. (1965), 'Reading Readiness', *Teacher of the Blind*, 53(3), pp. 95–9.

PLOWDEN REPORT (1967), see Central Advisory Council for Education.

PRITCHARD, D. G. (1963), *Education and the Handicapped 1760–1960*, Routledge & Kegan Paul, pp. 25–51.

RAFFLE, F. (1970), 'Are you Ready, Play', *Teacher of the Blind*, 58(3), pp. 58–60.

REYNELL, N. AND ZINKIN, P. (1975), 'New Procedures', *Child Care, Health and Development*, 5(1), pp. 61–9.

ROBINSON, D. P. (1975), 'Closed Circuit Television', *Teacher of the Blind*, 63(2), pp. 43–6.

ROYAL NATIONAL INSTITUTE FOR THE BLIND (undated), *Children with Severe Visual Handicap*.

SCHONELL, F. T. (1948), *Backwardness in the Basic Subjects*, Oliver & Boyd.

SHANNON, W. (1971), 'Mobility Training in Schools for the Visually Handicapped', *Teacher of the Blind*, 60(1), pp. 25–30.

SHAW, A. (1969), *Print for Partial Sight*, Research Report, Library Association.

SHEPERDSON, K. L. (1967), 'Deprivation: A Study of Sighted Children of Blind Parents', *New Beacon*, 51(607), pp. 283–8.

SHERIDAN, M. D. (1969), *Manual for the Stycar Vision Tests*, National Foundation for Educational Research.

SILVER, J. AND GOULD, E. (1976), 'A Study of Some Factors Concerned in the Schooling of Visually Handicapped Children', *Child Care, Health and Development*, 2(3), pp. 145–53.

SIMON, G. B. AND LEARY, J. (1972), *Investigation into the Behaviour and Needs of Visually Handicapped and Mentally Retarded Children in an Experimental Residential and Educational Unit*, Research Centre for the Education of the Visually Handicapped, University of Birmingham, pp. 1–14.

SIMS, A. M. (1967), 'Modern Mathematics in a Secondary School', *The Teaching of Science and Mathematics to the Blind*, Royal National Institute for the Blind.

SMITH, V. H. (1971), 'The Effects of Visual Handicap on Concept Formation', *Teacher of the Blind*, 59(2), pp. 53–61.

SMITH, V. H. AND JAMES, F. E. (1968), *Eyes and Education*, Heinemann Medical Books.

SOLNTSEVA, L. T. (1966), 'Features peculiar to perception of the blind pre-school child', *Mental Development and Sensory Defects*, 18th International Congress of Psychology, Moscow, pp. 226–30.

SOMMERS, V. S. (1944), *The Influence of Parental Attitudes and Social Environment on the Personality Development of the Adolescent Blind*, American Foundation for the Blind.

SORSBY, A. (1972), *Modern Ophthalmology*, Butterworths.

STEPHENS, B. (1972), 'Cognitive processes of the visually impaired', *Education of the Visually Handicapped*, 4(4), pp. 106–11.

SYKES, K. C. (1975), 'Print reading for visually handicapped children', Southern and Western Regional Association for the Blind, *Regional Review*, 59, pp. 1–5.

SYKES, K. C. (1977), 'Legibility of Print for Visually Impaired Children', *Teacher of the Blind*, 65(2), pp. 67–84.

TANSLEY, M. E. (1967), *Reading and Remedial Reading*, Routledge & Kegan Paul.

TANSLEY, M. E. AND NICHOLLS, K. M. (1962), *Racing to Read*, E. J. Arnold.

TAYLOR, D. (1975), 'The prevalence of visual handicaps in England and Wales', *Child Care, Health and Development*, 5(2), pp. 291–7.

THWAITES, B. (1970), *A Statement on the Present State of Change in Mathematics at Secondary Level*, Joint Mathematical Council, pp. 1–20.

TILLMAN, M. H. (1967), 'The performance of blind and sighted children on the Wechsler Intelligence Scale for Children', Study 2, *International Journal for the Education of the Blind*, 16, pp. 106–12.

TINKER, M. A. (1936), 'Eye movements in reading', *Journal of Educational Research*, no. 30, pp. 241–77.

TOBIN, M. J. (1971a), 'Report on overseas research', *Teacher of the Blind*, 59(3), pp. 117–26, 59(4), pp. 154–70.

TOBIN, M. J. (1971b), *Programmed Instruction and Braille Learning*, Research Centre for the Education of the Visually Handicapped, University of Birmingham.

TOBIN, M. J. (1972a), 'A study in the improvement of visual efficiency in children registered as blind', *New Beacon*, 56(659), pp. 58–60.

TOBIN, M. J. (1972b), *The Vocabulary of the Young Blind Schoolchild*, College of Teachers of the Blind.

TOBIN, M. J. (1972c), 'Conservation of substance in the blind and partially sighted', *British Journal of Educational Psychology*, 42(2), pp. 192–7.

TOBIN, M. J. (1977), *Testing the Blind and Partially Sighted*, Research Centre for the Education of the Visually Handicapped, University of Birmingham.

TOBIN, M. J., HILL, R. E., LEARY, J. AND SIMON, G. B., *Investigations into the Behaviour and Needs of Visually handicapped and Mentally Retarded Children in an Experimental Residential and Educational Unit*, Research Centre for the Education of the Visually Handicapped, University of Birmingham.

TOBIN, M. J., JAMES, W. R. K., MCVEIGH, A. AND IRVING, R. M. (1973), *Print Reading by the Blind: An Evaluation of the Optacon and an Investigation of Some Learner Variables and Teaching Methods*, Research Centre for the Education of the Visually Handicapped, University of Birmingham.

TOBIN, M. J. AND WILKINSON, A. M. (1972), *Aims and Methods in the Teaching of English to the Visually Handicapped*, Research Centre for the Education of the Visually Handicapped, University of Birmingham.

TOOZE, D. (1967), 'Mobility for the Junior Blind Child', *Teacher of the Blind*, 55(4), pp. 108–11.

TOOZE, D. (1972), *Mobility Training in Schools for the Visually Handicapped*, Working Party Conference on Mobility Training, College of Teachers of the Blind, pp. 7–10.

TOOZE, F. H. G. (1962), *Braille Speed Test*, College of Teachers of the Blind.

TOOZE, F. H. G. (1967), 'Mathematics for Primary School Blind Children', *The Teaching of Science and Mathematics to the Blind*, Royal National Institute for the Blind, pp. 62–106.

TROWALD, N. (1975), 'Learning strategies for blind listeners', Southern Regional Association for the Blind, *Report*, no. 66, pp. 115–27.

VAN DER ZWAN, J. L, AND HESLINGA, K. (1970), 'What Should we Teach?' *Teacher of the Blind*, 59, pp. 18–29.

VENN, E. J. (1964), 'Placement – Present Attitudes and Future Needs', *New Beacon*, 48(572), pp. 656–9.

VERNON, M. D. (1971), *Reading and its Difficulties*, Cambridge University Press.

VERNON REPORT (1972), see Department of Education and Science.

VINCENT, N. (1970), 'Perspective Drawing', *The Teaching of Science and Mathematics to the Blind*, Royal National Institute for the Blind, pp. 144–5.

WHITTAKER, J. (1967), 'Graphic Representation', *The Teaching of Science and Mathematics to the Blind*, Royal National Institute for the Blind, pp. 110–18.

WILLIAMS, C. E. (1967), 'Some factors in the aetiology of behaviour disorders of blind children', *Teacher of the Blind*, 56(1), pp. 18–24.

WILLIAMS, C. E. (1969), 'A unit for psychiatrically disturbed blind children', *Teacher of the Blind*, 58(2) pp. 64–6.

WILLIAMS, M. (1968), 'Superior intelligence of children with retinoblastoma', *Archives of Diseases of Childhood*, 43(228), April, pp. 204–10.

WILLIAMS, M. (1971), 'Braille Reading', *Teacher of the Blind*, 59(3), pp. 103–16.

WILLIAMS, M. (1973), *Stresses in Childhood* (ed. Varma), University of London Press, pp. 105–15.

WILLS, D. M. (1965), 'Some observations on blind nursery school children's understanding of their world', *Psychoanalytic Study of the Child*, 20, pp. 344–64.

WILSON, D. (1968), 'Horizon no. 5', *Listener*, 14 March, pp. 320–5.

WOLFFE, M. (1975), 'Employment and the Partially Sighted', *Eyepiece*, 1(4), pp. 2–4.

ZADIK, D. (1973), 'Social and Medical Aspects of the Battered Child with Vision Impairment', *New Outlook*, 67(6), pp. 241–50.

ZAHRAN, H. A. S. (1965), 'A Study of Personality Differences Between Blind and Sighted Children', *British Journal of Educational Psychology*, 3(35), pp. 329–37.

ZWEIBELSON, I. AND BORG, C. S. (1967), 'Concept development of blind children', *New Outlook*, 61, September, pp. 218–22.

Index